WHAT'S THE HURRY?

WHAT'S THE HURRY?

Developmental Activities for Able and Handicapped Children

by
Anne Rogovin, M.A.
Special Education Teacher

and
Christine Z. Cataldo, Ed.D.

Assistant Professor, Early Childhood Education, and
Director, Early Childhood Research Center,
S.U.N.Y. at Buffalo

UNIVERSITY PARK PRESS Baltimore

UNIVERSITY PARK PRESS
International Publishers in Science, Medicine, and Education
300 North Charles Street
Baltimore, Maryland 21201

Copyright © 1983 by University Park Press

Typeset by University Park Press, Typesetting Division
Manufactured in the United States of America by
The Maple Press Company

Photo Credits
Cover: Dr. Max Ronis
Still photos: Sherwin Greenberg and Frederick Marschall
Action photos: Milton Rogovin and Christine Cataldo

Library of Congress Cataloging in Publication Data

Rogovin, Anne.
What's the hurry.

1. Creative activities and seat work—Handbooks, manuals, etc.
2. Children—Books and reading—Handbooks, manuals, etc.
3. Child development—Handbooks, manuals, etc.
4. Handicapped children—Education—Handbooks, manuals, etc.
I. Cataldo, Christine Z. II. Title.
LB1537.R576   1982   372.13'07'8   82-13450
ISBN 0-8391-1761-2

CONTENTS

FOREWORD

In this age of rushing, of acceleration, of modifying curricula so as to introduce children to experiences at ever younger ages, it is refreshing to encounter a book that asks, "What's the Hurry?" One that reminds us that children themselves are in no hurry to stop exploring and manipulating and creating and learning about people, objects, and events in an integrated and totally committed way. One that demonstrates that the most effective teaching materials are available at little cost to the creative teacher or parent. And one based on the premise that teaching-learning activities that are matched to a child's developmental level will appeal to either normal or handicapped children.

The activities described and pictured in this book have been developed by Anne Rogovin over a quarter of a century devoted to teaching normal and handicapped children. Her love of and devotion to children shine through everything she does and every book she writes, as will be attested to by those who have read her previous books. She has a special talent for designing creative teaching techniques that can be made from inexpensive and readily available materials. The ones she has designed and made are appealing to children and hold their attention effectively while allowing an array of skills to develop.

Materials can occasionally create an eclectic nightmare and lead to confused and unsystematic utilization in the teaching program. Not so with the teaching materials described in this book, for Christine Cataldo has anchored them in a solid framework of developmental theory. From this collaboration has come a whole which will be more meaningful to educators than the sum of the two separate parts. The teaching exercises are organized into three main areas of development—physical, personal, and intellectual—with instructions provided for basic levels of achievement, followed by variations that allow teachers to embellish the exercises and not feel constrained by an instructional paradigm proposed by the authors. This type of flexibility is an absolute necessity for any such curriculum guide, as creative teachers find instructional formulae that call for slavish adherence to a preset routine, an anathema. This will most certainly *not* be the reaction to these exercises and the text that accompanies them.

In making a final promise to readers of this book I have to fall back on some rather unprofessional language—words like *down-to-earth, practical, warm,* and *charming.* You will find yourselves smiling as you read the text and look at the delightful photographs that illustrate each exercise. You will occasionally lament, "Now why didn't I think of that myself?" Regardless, you will recognize the value of this approach to facilitating the development of young children and be glad you discovered the book and the ideas of its authors.

Bettye M. Caldwell
Distinguished Professor of Education
University of Arkansas at Little Rock

PREFACE

All of us want our children to grow to be healthy, productive, independent citizens of society; but it isn't always easy in this restless, hurried world of ours, especially when we see how television, radio, movies, books, magazines—and people, too—seem to inundate children with hurried, "instant" information and ways.

How many times have you seen a child totally absorbed in something, interrupted by a "hurry up" command? It might be an audible one, or it might be just a "look." But the child knows very well what it means. The child may not be able to verbalize it, but have you ever seen this child *look* as if to say:

> *Please don't hurry me...*
> *Let me go slow...*
> *Let me look at things...*
> *Let me touch and handle things...*
> *Let me hear and smell and maybe*
> *taste some things...*
> *I just know I can learn many*
> *things—in time...*
> *If you'll only let me go at my own*
> *speed in my own*
> *way—please...*

I have seen (and perhaps you have, too) classes of "normal" children and/or those with handicapping conditions hurried from one new lesson to a second, then on to the third—without a solid foundation of the first *or* second. The result is a foundation that is not solid, that may crumble apart with confusion and uncertainties until the child says, "I can't" or "I don't want to."

As a special class teacher for almost 30 years (and incidentally, mother of three children who are also teachers), I have always worried that some of these children might miss out on other ways of learning—

> *ways that are slower, but more*
> *lasting*
> *ways that are real, and become a*
> *part of their hearts and minds*
> *ways that are just for early*
> *childhood*
> *ways that cannot wait, for childhood*
> *goes by quickly, and there is no*
> *going back*

You may care to know how my materials came about. I'm not really 100% sure myself, but I think it may have had something to do with the fact that store-bought, ready-made, "instant" things never seemed right for my classes. Instead of the materials being simple and big so they could be easily understood and easily handled by not too well coordinated hands and fingers, they usually turned out to be too small, too hard to understand, too hard to follow, and (in the end) got put aside or got lost.

In the decades of my work, I have found several important ingredients for learning, one of which is that very precious feeling of confidence in oneself, that "I can do it." If a child has this feeling, there seems to be no stops. Hurdles are licked. Mountains are climbed. The sky is the limit. But if this precious feeling is never gotten or is damaged or lost, demoralization and failure set in, become entrenched, and the delicious fruits of learning decay. Confidence is basic to all the activities in *What's the Hurry?*, but there are several other special features.

In going through the pages, you will notice that most of the projects seem very easy and fun for the child to do. It really isn't of much significance that a blind child be able to put a chestnut in a hole. It *is* significant that this child picks up a chestnut, finds the hole, drops the chestnut in the hole, and feels, "Gee, that was fun...I'll do another one." Then the child does it again, and again, each time accumulating small successes and added confidence in oneself.

When a toddler hunts for a red sock to match with another red sock and finds it, proclaiming (either inwardly or loud and clear), "I got it! I got it all by myself!"—see how willingly the child will want to match the blues with the blues, the yellows with the yellows. Squares with squares. Circles with circles. Knives, forks, and spoons.

Instead of using drawings or photographs, we need *concrete* objects that are relevant and important to the children's lives *now*. (And, when you stop to think about it, *it* really isn't must different from we as adults, who—when we want to do something—usually can do it faster.) We need:

> *Real* shoes for matching
> *Real* buttons to sort into colors or
>   make into a pretty necklace
> *Real* locks to learn how they work
> *Real* bells that ring
> *Real* keys to put on hooks
> *Real* pennies, nickels, and dimes to
>   play store with

The concept of "in and out" is joyfully learned by putting soda cans "in and out" of a wooden case. When "in and out" are learned well, the child will not have to be prodded to learn "up and down," "inside and outside," or "under and over."

We need real things that have to do with nature, for it seems to me there ought to be a sympathy with nature, a kind of harmony with our environment, an understanding that nature (despite the pollution and the crowded cities) is all around us, sending out messages to us, begging us to *pay attention.*

As you go through the pages, you will come across some "books." I call them "Look, Touch, Say Books" because that's just what they are. You can *look* at them, *touch* them, and/or *say* "what they are."

You can see that they aren't the usual books you buy in stores, books with printed words on fine snowy white paper, bound and glued. These are very *special books for little children* who like to "read" long before their young years are ready for abstract thinking. The best part is, you can make the books by yourself, or (better yet) you can make them *with* your child, or your child can make them *"all by myself."*

Let your child pick out a book to which he or she seems inclined. Will it be the Round Book? Does the Large and Small Book strike his or her fancy? How about the Pennies Book? Or the one of Pairs?

Don't worry about the pages getting banged up. They are made of cardboard which is sturdy and just right for not too careful hands. You can "read" one page at a time—plopping one on your lap, on the table, or sprawled out on the floor. Or you can stand all the pages up against the back of the livingroom couch to "read". Don't you think the Light and Dark Book might look good enough to exhibit on the kitchen or bedroom wall?

See how each book has one special "story"— things that are pertinent and related to the child's environment, things that have to do with eating, dressing, colors, nature. When the child has a solid understanding of these things, he or she begins to "feel good," developing a kind of inner security that makes the child want to find out about other things and how much more eyes can be *taught to see.*

> *Improvise*—and, just like with most other things—
> the more you *improvise,* the better you get at it
> *Take off*
> and
> *Fly,* using your own creativity that all of us
have when we need it
> *Have fun*
> *Enjoy yourself*
> for
> **What's the Hurry?**

Anne Rogovin

ACKNOWLEDGMENTS

These materials would never have been possible without

All of my students who forced me to find enticing ways to reach them so their learning would be fun—and so, easier for them

The support and help of my ever-patient husband, Milton

Some friends, including custodians of schools where I taught who didn't know how to say "no" whenever I needed technical help for electrical connections and such things

Dr. Clifford Crooks (Superintendent of the Board of Cooperative Education Services #1), who believed in my work and helped me get two Sabbatical Leaves of Absence from my teaching

A special thanks to Michael Begab of University Park Press for his confidence in *What's the Hurry?* and his gentle wisdom in "fathering" it toward its successful completion.

Anne Rogovin

The author acknowledges and appreciates the help and support of the staff and families at the Early Childhood Research Center, SUNY at Buffalo, and the Cantalician Center for Learning, Buffalo, New York. Especially appreciated is the work of Joan Jengo, Center secretary, and the advice of Michael Begab of University Park Press in the completion of this manuscript.

Christine Z. Cataldo

Editor's Note

All of the materials described and photographed in
What's the Hurry? were created by Anne Rogovin.

The text and curriculum suggestions were written by
Christine Cataldo.

To my dearest husband and comrade, Milton
  Our children
    Ellen (and her husband, Jack)
    Mark
    Paula (and her husband, Peter)
  Their children
    David
    Malaika
    Steven
    Aliya
    Eric
And all the children on the earth—that they grow to be healthy and productive in a world of peace and friendship.

A. R.

To my family,
  Jerry, Jason, and Claudia

C. Z. C.

INTRODUCTION

THE DEVELOPMENTAL PROCESS

The materials presented in this text are intended to serve as a medium for supporting the developmental process; that is, the activities serve as challenges to develop and reinforce particular skills and understandings. The learnings that are described are known to be important to children's progress along a continuum of growth and learning from early to later abilities. Each of the 88 materials presented in this text has been "assigned" to a primary area of development and an approximate level of difficulty. It is expected that the child who uses that activity will grow in skill, competence, and personal confidence in that area of development at about that level. The result is that children are quite enjoyably guided through developmental stages at their own individual pace with interesting, active, self-learning materials.

THE DEVELOPMENTAL AREAS

The area-ability distinctions used here, although meaningful, are nonetheless open to question. This is because such levels and areas become quite blurred when they are actually used with children. It is not surprising that this happens because development is, in fact, more complicated, more multifaceted and unpredictable than any of our descriptions of it. We can try to describe the sequence, but each individual child proceeds unevenly through the stages. Toddlers and preschoolers always show pockets of strengths and needs; handicapped youngsters demonstrate quite unique patterns of disabilities and capabilities. For many of these children there is growth and change in response to the youngster's interest, motivation, and sheer delight in a particular challenge. Teachers and parents

must, therefore, be vigilant and use their own observation and judgment about such developmental guidelines.

In making these materials available for the child's pleasure and learning, the teacher, aide, or parent should make an effort to leave the child's activity options open; that is, although you do not want to select too frustrating an activity for a child, you need to avoid underestimates of ability that occur when you prejudge the child's limitations. It may be helpful to think of readiness as a process of adult alertness to real and specific skills and interests in children. You apply tasks at common levels across domains, and then look for the child's responses. This works better than the straightforward use of global age and stage categories. You might call this a progressive approach to development, one that reflects some sequencing but relies primarily upon the child's own scattered progress along a developmental continuum; this observed progress determines readiness for increasingly more difficult experiences. These are, after all, self-learning materials. Their value comes partly from the child's own pacing of his or her individual development, which results when you let the child's ability and interest shape his or her learning sequence.

STRATEGIES

In view of these principles, the most useful strategy for relating *What's the Hurry?* activities to growth may be to try out an array of simple and complex materials in each area, then observe the child's approaches to them. Look especially for signs of strong motivation to succeed and for reactions such as a child's delight and persistence. These reactions may produce success with otherwise difficult materials; they will also protect the vulnerable child from failure because you can backtrack if an activity is too challenging. *What's the Hurry?* is, as you can see, an important phrase for helping children move gradually through the developmental process. Taking the time to try, to do, to think, ensures that the child plays an active role, much like the principles described by Montessori and Piaget, in determining their own level and pace of learning and development. To build lasting skills and promote enduring understandings, use these materials and activities to give the children the time, space, and opportunity to seek and enjoy their own unique challenges.

SUGGESTIONS FOR ORGANIZING MATERIALS

For each of three major areas of development identified in Table 1 (physical, personal, and intellectual) a table is presented at the beginning of that section of the book.

levels as well. This was a deliberate feature of their design! The philosophy we used is that *multipurpose* or integrated activities are capable of promoting deeper understandings and wider abilities than most activities with a single focus. The *multilevel* approach may similarly lead to building up a range of competencies across several ability levels. In the scheme we used here, age categories have been avoided in favor of levels of uses of the materials. The levels go from exploration or simple challenges to mastery (moderate difficulty), variations (special ideas or unique challenges), and advanced or complex challenges.

When you organize the materials across a period of time (i.e., the school year), it is suggested that children begin by working with the simplest materials in each of the large areas of development. Activities from *each* of the three subsections of that developmental area should be used. They also represent different types of ability, but, more importantly, they reflect the diversity within each developmental area. The learning program you implement may

Table 1. Overview of *What's the Hurry?* activities, developmental areas, and difficulty levels

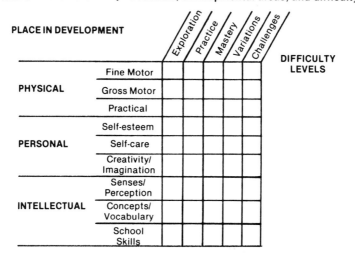

The tables place each of the learning materials and suggested activities in subcategories of the particular developmental area and in one of five levels of difficulty. It is important to note, however, that most items can be placed in other areas and

very well be a richer one for this built-in variability of learning area and level.

As already discussed, the materials have been arranged in accordance with characteristics of the developmental process. We used this format to emphasize the role of the activity in the developmental process, but there are also distinct types of materials that could be reorganized by *function*. There are boards, hooks, trays, and boxes. There are lottos, books, sorting tasks, drop-in tasks, sensory experiences, and arrangements. Some are especially appropriate for severely handicapped children; others are designed for competent preschoolers. As teachers, aides, and parents begin to build a curriculum around these materials and activities, they may want to use more than one organizing framework. Whatever style you use, there is enough variety to help you implement a series of learning activities that fits your teaching style.

THE PICTURE PAGES

When the 88 *What's the Hurry?* materials were arranged into three areas of development, we decided to introduce the area with words and with pictures. The "picture pages" are a series of photographs depicting aspects of the physical, personal, and intellectual areas of development. They show children engaged with the appropriate materials. You might want to take a close look at these to gain a feeling for the children's enthusiasm for learning with hands-on materials and to help you better understand sequences in that particular area.

I. PHYSICAL AREA OF DEVELOPMENT

Certainly, for all young and/or handicapped children the physical area of growth is somewhat easy to observe and quite necessary to work with. The challenges presented to the child must, however, be appropriate, safe, and relevant. For the confined youngster, it may be particularly important to provide activities that result in success and learning. For the very young, mastery of the physical world is very closely tied to personal and intellectual growth. Materials 1 to 27 fall into this domain.

The fine motor area includes the child's use of fingers and hands to manipulate smaller materials. At this point in development it is important to build a sequence of successes in this physical area that creates feelings of confidence. The ability to learn from other materials requiring fine motor skills will later expand the child's skills in several academic areas. The gross motor area involves arm movements as well. These make it possible for severely handicapped and very young children to bring some muscles under control yet manage to be successful. In the practical domain, the child applies growing physical skills to simple, daily challenges. Practicing these activities is a delightful way to build confidence and skills closely tied to family life and school independence.

PHYSICAL AREA

Aspects of Physical Development

Levels of difficulty[a]	Fine Motor (using fingers and hands)	Gross Motor (using hands and arms)	Practical (everyday tasks)
Exploration (simple challenges)	1 / Hanging Bracelets 2 / Silverware Hooking	13 / Wheel Box 14 / Bucket Ball	20 / Door Opener 21 / Doorbell
Practice (a bit harder)	3 / Washers for Show 4 / Pegs in a Row 5 / Chip Drop	15 / Chime and Bell Boxes 16 / Baskets and Cans	22 / Light Switches 23 / Shoe Shop
Mastery (moderate challenges)	6 / Sticks and Squares 7 / Threads and Hooks 8 / Spoons and Brushes	17 / Dropping Box: Caps and Nuts	24 / Table Setting 25 / Door and Key Latches
Variations (special challenges)	9 / Pencils in Place 10 / Clothespin Stand	18 / Display Trays: Silverware, Buttons, and Pennies	26 / Telephone Dial
Complex challenges (difficult tasks)	11 / Dozens of Tops 12 / Key Hangings	19 / Sort and Hang: Mittens, Socks, and Cloths	27 / Bike Lock

[a]These are approximated; each child's task varies according to his or her particular physical condition and interests.

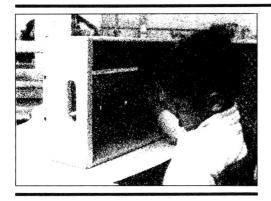

1 HANGING BRACELETS

AREA

Physical: Fine Motor

PURPOSE

To explore and try a simple fine motor task.

Place in Development

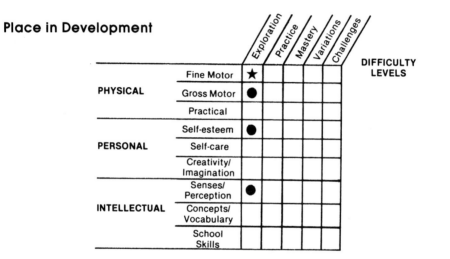

		Exploration	Practice	Mastery	Variations	Challenges
				DIFFICULTY LEVELS		
PHYSICAL	Fine Motor	★				
	Gross Motor	●				
	Practical					
PERSONAL	Self-esteem	●				
	Self-care					
	Creativity/ Imagination					
INTELLECTUAL	Senses/ Perception	●				
	Concepts/ Vocabulary					
	School Skills					

Other Areas: Gross Motor

Specific Value

Large, smooth rings, a sturdy box, and open hooks make this physical task one that is relatively simple to manage and highly satisfying when achieved. The visual effect of the rings placed on the hooks provides, in addition, lots of good feelings when the child is successful. The task also promotes persistence in that children who learn continued efforts can achieve a goal. For many youngsters, practicing and refining eye, hand, and arm coordination with these materials serves to prepare them for more difficult challenges.

Child's Readiness

For toddlers and moderately handicapped children this activity is very appropriate early in their experience.

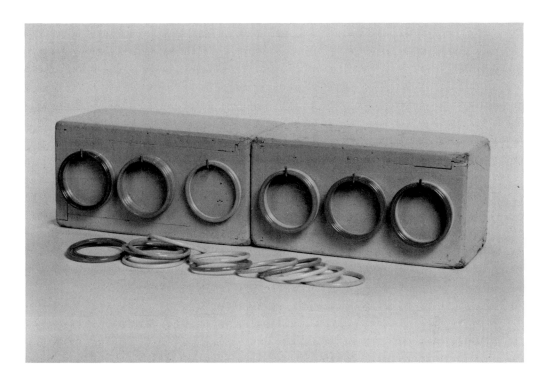

Applications

Very young children will enjoy this greatly because they can see the product — a neat row of attractive circles.

Children with coordination problems can still succeed with these materials because the rings are so large.

Variations and Related Ideas

Colored plastic bracelets are delightful additions to this activity, as are those with different shapes, textures, and materials. At the same time children may attempt to put bracelets on their arms or on ropes or sticks. In all these instances, they are practicing important physical skills, and extended use of the materials should be encouraged.

Comments

Be sure the hooks used here are not too sharp at the edges or too close to the board.

2 SILVERWARE HOOKING

AREA

Physical: Fine Motor

PURPOSE

To work at hanging up familiar everyday materials.

Place in Development

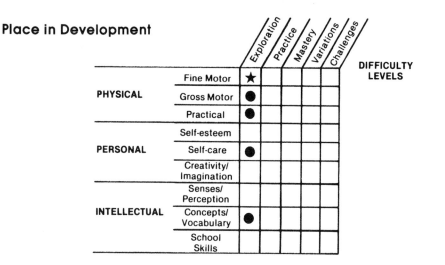

		Exploration	Practice	Mastery	Variations	Challenges	DIFFICULTY LEVELS
PHYSICAL	Fine Motor	★					
	Gross Motor	●					
	Practical	●					
PERSONAL	Self-esteem						
	Self-care	●					
	Creativity/ Imagination						
INTELLECTUAL	Senses/ Perception						
	Concepts/ Vocabulary	●					
	School Skills						

Other Areas: Gross Motor

Specific Value

This simple, straightforward task requires the coordination of fingers, hands, and arms to display the silverware successfully on small hooks. The use of forks, spoons, and knives is very deliberate; they are common and comfortable for children to handle. For many youngsters this use of concrete and familiar items provides a good deal of motivation to succeed. Even though the rings are small and require effort to negotiate, the long handles on the silverware pieces make the task a bit easier than those with smaller hand grips.

Child's Readiness

This is a beginning motor task, yet one that can challenge children needing to bring their muscles under control.

Applications

The familiarity of these utensils will attract the very young who enjoy everyday materials.

Moderately physically handicapped youngsters will enjoy this challenge.

Variations and Related Ideas

Children may enjoy changing the displays they create with these materials—from all of a kind to a one-of-each table setting. They may also be able to play a Hide and Seek or What's Missing game by taking away an item or covering it up and remembering what's gone.

Comments

Be certain to choose very smooth-edged forks and knives. You may also need to remind children not to put their mouths on the utensils.

3 WASHERS FOR SHOW

AREA

Physical: Fine Motor

PURPOSE

To practice a motor task using sets of materials with interesting textures.

Place in Development

		Exploration	Practice	Mastery	Variations	Challenges
PHYSICAL	Fine Motor		★			
	Gross Motor	●	●			
	Practical					
PERSONAL	Self-esteem					
	Self-care					
	Creativity/ Imagination		●			
INTELLECTUAL	Senses/ Perception		●			
	Concepts/ Vocabulary					
	School Skills					

DIFFICULTY LEVELS

Other Areas: Gross Motor; Sensory Perception

Specific Value

Sets of like materials often seem to challenge children to organize and use them repeatedly. It may be that this form of practice satisfies their need to get involved in a task and persist until it has clearly been finished. The sets of soft and hard washers—each interesting in its own way—arouse the child's curiosity, making the task even more pleasurable. Because arms, hands, fingers, and eyes are involved, the child who works with the materials should gain in the coordination and use of these muscle groups.

Child's Readiness

Because there are sets of materials, this task is slightly more difficult than those with fewer materials, yet the child with beginning motor skills should find it appropriate.

Applications

Young children will enjoy touching and feeling these sets of rings; they are lots of fun.

Blind and cerebral palsied children should appreciate this interesting challenge that is still within their ability.

Variations and Related Ideas

The heavy blocks on which these hooks are placed makes it possible for children to bump against them without disturbing what they have already accomplished. Other racks can be used later, such as coat or cup racks. Counting games can be added as children remove the rings; children can also sort the washers by size.

Comments

The smaller washers shown here may be too difficult for some children to pick up; if this is true, or if the children are very young, then the larger, fatter washers should be used.

4 PEGS IN A ROW

AREA

Physical: Fine Motor

PURPOSE

To practice eye-hand coordination with large pegs.

Place in Development

		Exploration	Practice	Mastery	Variations	Challenges	DIFFICULTY LEVELS
PHYSICAL	Fine Motor	★					
	Gross Motor						
	Practical						
PERSONAL	Self-esteem	●					
	Self-care						
	Creativity/ Imagination						
INTELLECTUAL	Senses/ Perception		●				
	Concepts/ Vocabulary						
	School Skills						

Other Areas: Sensory Perception

Specific Value

Most pegs and peg boards are too small or too complicated for young and handi-capped children. Pegs in a Row is visually pleasing and large enough to produce a successful experience for the child with beginning coordination skills. It involves perceptual skills as well. With frequent use, children are able to quickly line up pegs and systematically place them in their holes. There is also a great deal of motivation to practice and persist in filling each of these parts in the row.

Child's Readiness

Children with relatively little experience and ability can attempt this task with at least some trial-and-error success. Later, they will achieve success more regularly.

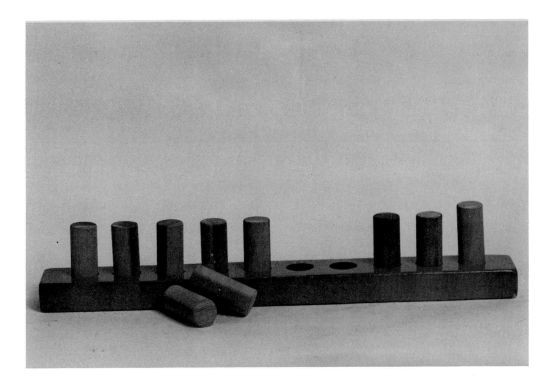

Applications

Toddlers adore this kind of arrangement of the same items in a row!
This is a fine practice activity for the child who is propped for sitting.

Variations and Related Ideas

Because there are 10 pegs and spaces, the children may be able to compare them to 10 fingers and 10 toes! Stacking and rolling activities might be interesting variations that the child can create, practice and learn from, such as five stacks of two each or rolling-in-a-box contests.

Comments

Some children even liken these round, smooth pegs to families—especially if they find a bigger "parent" peg and one or two slightly smaller "children" pegs!

5 CHIP DROP

AREA

Physical: Fine Motor

PURPOSE

To practice grasping, placing and releasing small objects.

Place in Development

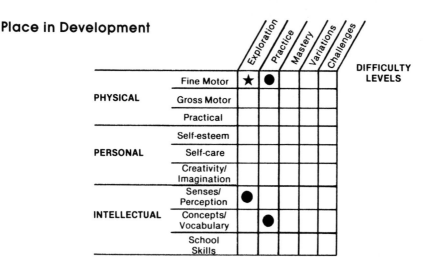

		Exploration	Practice	Mastery	Variations	Challenges	DIFFICULTY LEVELS
PHYSICAL	Fine Motor	★	●				
	Gross Motor						
	Practical						
PERSONAL	Self-esteem						
	Self-care						
	Creativity/ Imagination						
INTELLECTUAL	Senses/ Perception	●					
	Concepts/ Vocabulary		●				
	School Skills						

Other Areas: Intellectual

Specific Value

The "clink" of a disk as it drops into a wood or metal container provides a sense of satisfaction and reinforcement—it says success! There are some fine-motor coordination skills involved here because the round chip has to be fitted into a corresponding slot (definitely enlarged to make it easier). When the child releases it, he or she is using muscle control and mentally anticipating a result while also understanding a cause-and-effect relationship where one particular action leads to a consequence. This, then, is a form of thinking and reasoning that is enhanced through body activity.

Child's Readiness

Once the child is able to pick up and hold the thin disk or chip, he or she will most likely be able to manage this activity.

Applications

Toddlers also love the disappearing quality of this material, and it appears in another place. How fascinating!

Blind youngsters and those confined to chairs will enjoy this "noisy" task.

Variations and Related Ideas

Any set of small (but pleasant to handle) objects can be used for the Chip Drop. They should, however, make a solid sound on impact, because this stimulates anticipation. Counting activities can be added at an appropriate point. So, too, can simple two-person games such as My Turn-Your Turn, or Let's Race to the Finish.

Comments

Taking the chips out of the drop box and replacing them into the storage can is part of the task.

6 STICKS AND SQUARES

AREA

Physical: Fine Motor

PURPOSE

To master a sorting, stacking, and visual-motor task.

Place in Development

		Exploration	Practice	Mastery	Variations	Challenges
PHYSICAL	Fine Motor			★		
	Gross Motor					
	Practical					
PERSONAL	Self-esteem					
	Self-care					
	Creativity/ Imagination					
INTELLECTUAL	Senses/ Perception	●				
	Concepts/ Vocabulary	●				
	School Skills					

DIFFICULTY LEVELS

Other Areas: Sensory Discrimination

Specific Value

Taken together, matching and stacking activities help to develop children's coordination of the physical and mental modes of learning. With these materials the child focuses on locating the correct colors and sizes of squares, then placing them together with others on the matching stick. "Mistakes" are noted quickly by the discrepant color or shape. Physically, the child has some latitude in being able to move squares several times over the stick until the hole is discovered.

Child's Readiness

Sufficient physical coordination skills are needed here to prevent frustration.

Applications

Preschoolers will embrace the color-shape-number concepts here, trying each in turn.

Retarded children can rehearse this activity and learn some colors and amounts as well.

Variations and Related Ideas

Children may wish to use the squares without sticks, or they may wish to experiment with mixing colors and sizes. Very capable youngsters may even be able to produce consistent patterns or series of colors on a stick. Counting games can be played where one color has to match another. Squares can also be threaded onto a rope just for the fun and challenge.

Comments

The bigger the hole (and wider the stick), the easier this activity will be for some children. Fewer squares can also be used. Young children may not handle the sticks safely, so you may need to be sure they are seated first.

7 THREADS AND HOOKS

AREA

Physical: Fine Motor

PURPOSE

To attempt to place objects on "indirect" hooks.

Place in Development

		Exploration	Practice	Mastery	Variations	Challenges
PHYSICAL	Fine Motor			★	●	
	Gross Motor			●		
	Practical					
PERSONAL	Self-esteem					
	Self-care					
	Creativity/ Imagination		●			
INTELLECTUAL	Senses/ Perception		●			
	Concepts/ Vocabulary					
	School Skills					

DIFFICULTY LEVELS

Other Areas: Gross Motor

Specific Value

To negotiate the hooks and spaces on these colorful spools of thread requires children to fit them together without clearly seeing the parts. That is, the hole is on the bottom of the spool, out of sight, and the child has to "feel" where and how to move his or her arm. Regardless of this extra, built-in challenge, children enjoy handling these familiar materials that may already have been encountered in similar kinds of displays at home or in a fabric shop. The colors add a warm and interesting dimension, enabling the children to create a different visual display each time they use the materials.

Child's Readiness

This activity is moderately challenging for the child in that some coordination is needed for success.

Applications

Older preschoolers will enjoy these real spools and subtle differences in colors. Confined youngsters may appreciate working with this challenge at a table or on a lap.

Variations and Related Ideas

Spools of thread are fun to use whether they are filled or empty. They can be stacked like building blocks or they can be threaded on colorful strings or elastic. All of these activities promote better eye, hand, and arm coordinations and children's own variations.

Comments

Spools often have threads hanging. Clear nail polish can be used to contain threads on these spools; however, children can also learn from repeated attempts to affix the threads to their slits.

8 SPOONS AND BRUSHES

AREA

Physical: Fine Motor

PURPOSE

To master placing varying tall thin spoons and brushes into holes.

Place in Development

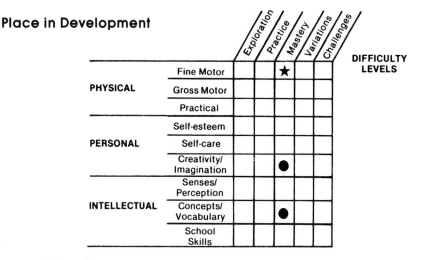

		Exploration	Practice	Mastery	Variations	Challenges
PHYSICAL	Fine Motor			★		
	Gross Motor					
	Practical					
PERSONAL	Self-esteem					
	Self-care					
	Creativity/ Imagination		●			
INTELLECTUAL	Senses/ Perception					
	Concepts/ Vocabulary		●			
	School Skills					

DIFFICULTY LEVELS

Other Areas: Intellectual: Concepts

Specific Value

The fitting of sets of similar objects into holes pleases children because of the immediate satisfaction that is felt each time this is achieved. In this case, the use of smooth wooden spoons of similar shape (but assorted sizes) brings a special appeal. The child who is able to get the pencil-like handle in its place is building important eye-hand coordination skills needed for later activities with pencils, scissors, pegs, etc. Perceptual skills are also practiced when the child makes arrangements by size or type of spoon. Real spoons and brushes reflect the real world. This makes the activity particularly appealing to the child. When the child enjoys and persists, the learning grows.

Child's Readiness

Children who are able to hold and place objects into containers (crayons, shape boxes, puzzle pieces) will also have adequate coordination for spoons and brushes. In the beginning, use a few spoons or brushes to simplify the activity—add more later.

Applications

The young child relates very well to many kinds of objects and containers. The spoons here are safe and sturdy.

Physically handicapped children may find this particularly satisfying and rewarding.

Variations and Related Ideas

Many different safe objects can be used, and the numbers and sizes of holes can be varied (the smaller, the more difficult). Cardboard and plastic can be substituted for the wood holder. Cardboard boxes can also be used. Assorted sizes and textures make the activity even more interesting, as do "used" objects with interesting imperfections.

Comments

It is important to let the child choose the number of spoons and the style used to place them into the holes. Persistence is important, but adults should give the child wide latitude in how this material is used.

9 PENCILS AND PLACES

AREA

Physical: Fine Motor

PURPOSE

To attempt a special challenge requiring eye-hand coordination.

Place in Development

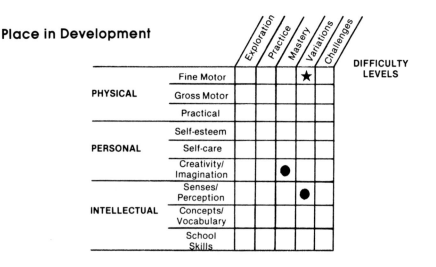

		Exploration	Practice	Mastery	Variations	Challenges	DIFFICULTY LEVELS
PHYSICAL	Fine Motor				★		
	Gross Motor						
	Practical						
PERSONAL	Self-esteem						
	Self-care						
	Creativity/ Imagination		●				
INTELLECTUAL	Senses/ Perception				●		
	Concepts/ Vocabulary						
	School Skills						

Other Areas: Creativity; Sensory Experiences

Specific Value

This delightful series of holes and corresponding objects will immediately attract children. It is more complicated than activities with fewer materials; in fact, the abundance of items to arrange here makes it a bit different in nature. It becomes somewhat creative—some pencils are up, some down, some are thinner or fatter, older or newer, and of varying colors. The motivation for children comes partly from exercising judgment about the specific use made of their coordination skills. It is also a practical task, i.e., putting pencils and scissors away.

Child's Readiness

Because there are many small holes and objects, this activity will both satisfy and challenge children able to grasp and direct their reach.

Applications

Toddlers and preschoolers enjoy these sorting-fitting-displaying materials. They are easy to manage and satisfying in effect.

Physically handicapped youngsters, especially those confined to chairs, will be able to practice important skills such as visually directed coordination skills.

Variations and Related Ideas

In addition to pencils and scissors, both of which are interesting and familiar, children can use colored dowels, sticks, plastic spoons, and any other slender materials. A great many pre-math activities can be created for children here, from counting-up to duplicating patterns of full or empty spaces. In fact, the more this material is used, the more ideas emerge for extending the learning.

Comments

Although children respond well to sets of like materials, they also appreciate some diversity within these, for example, unusual markings on a twig. It helps them attend to detail and notice similarities and differences.

10 CLOTHESPIN STAND

AREA

Physical: Fine Motor

PURPOSE

To apply eye-hand-arm coordination skills to an unusual challenge.

Place in Development

		Exploration	Practice	Mastery	Variations	Challenges	
							DIFFICULTY LEVELS
PHYSICAL	Fine Motor				★		
	Gross Motor				●		
	Practical						
PERSONAL	Self-esteem						
	Self-care						
	Creativity/ Imagination		●				
INTELLECTUAL	Senses/ Perception						
	Concepts/ Vocabulary						
	School Skills						

Other Areas: Gross Motor; Self-esteem

Specific Value

A good deal of strength and dexterity in the fingers is needed to manage opening a spring clothespin. Yet children enjoy the challenge partly because of the satisfaction they feel in observing how they can affect the opening and closing of the object. This activity contains two sorts of clothespins—the slip-on and clip varieties. If the child has difficulty succeeding with one, there is less effort needed with the other. Finger muscles can be strengthened considerably using either type.

Child's Readiness

The Clothespin Stand is a dual-level activity so that children can enjoy it if they are more or less able to coordinate these body parts.

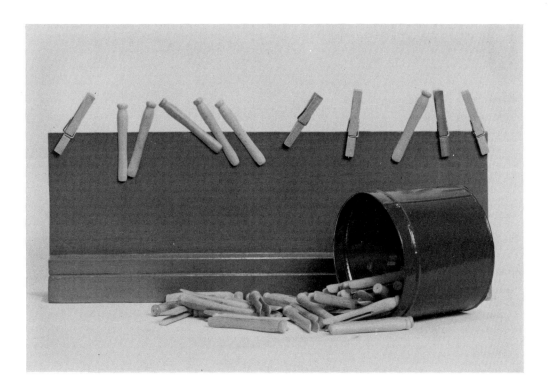

Applications

> Young children will appreciate the smooth wood and sturdy springs of the clothespins.
>
> Physically capable retarded children may enjoy this challenge because it requires mostly physical skills.

Variations and Related Ideas

> Children who delight in making displays of objects and materials may enjoy using the Clothespin Stand for other purposes. Folded pictures, doll clothing, giant paper clips, lengths of yarn—these can all be placed on the stand. They give a sense of satisfaction to the child. For imaginative children, a clothesline placed in the dollhouse area of the room will easily be incorporated into dramatic play involving washing and hanging clothes.

Comments

> You may need to watch out for accidentally clipped fingers when children first use the spring clothespins.

11 DOZENS OF TOPS

AREA

Physical: Fine Motor

PURPOSE

To attempt a challenging fine motor task.

Place in Development

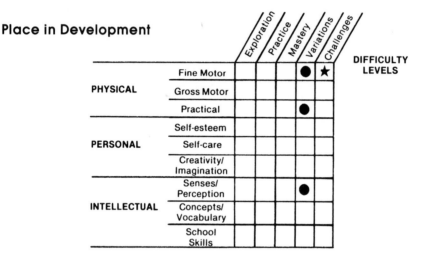

		Exploration	Practice	Mastery	Variations	Challenges	
PHYSICAL	Fine Motor				●	★	**DIFFICULTY LEVELS**
	Gross Motor						
	Practical			●			
PERSONAL	Self-esteem						
	Self-care						
	Creativity/ Imagination						
INTELLECTUAL	Senses/ Perception			●			
	Concepts/ Vocabulary						
	School Skills						

Other Areas: Sensory Experiences; Practical

Specific Value

The act of screwing a small top onto a can is a difficult one, yet an important task for children to achieve. To make it appealing and manageable, use this array of 12 anchored film cans with their colorful matching tops. Children will delight in removing all of the tops, then replacing them one by one. The screwing action required is a wonderful challenge; a brief turn is needed, but it is easy to succeed. The fun is partly in using three-dimensional rows of anchored objects.

Child's Readiness

This activity qualifies as a complex challenge because several physical skills are needed. It is so appealing, however, that it might be used well by any child interested in the task.

Applications

This array of off-on containers will charm the preschooler who delights in such a straightforward challenge.

The confined handicapped child can use this material for a variety of purposes all at one sitting.

Variations and Related Ideas

If children enjoy and succeed with this set of same-color lids and cans, they may later appreciate developing the activity into one requiring the matching of colors, alphabet letters, or numerals on cans and lids. You might also use the cans as surprise boxes, with small objects inside that the children can remember or try to find. Because these are metal, they will make a pleasant sound if beans or pebbles are dropped inside. It is also a challenge to the fingers and hands in retrieving them!

Comments

You might need to keep extra can tops hidden away in case one is lost. Having all of the tops on at once is an important reward for a job well done!

12 KEY HANGINGS

AREA

Physical: Fine Motor

PURPOSE

To use fingers and hands to organize keys in patterns and attend to details.

Place in Development

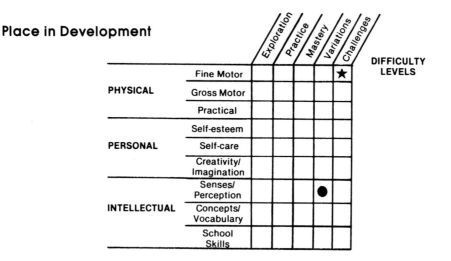

		Exploration	Practice	Mastery	Variations	Challenges
PHYSICAL	Fine Motor					★
	Gross Motor					
	Practical					
PERSONAL	Self-esteem					
	Self-care					
	Creativity/ Imagination					
INTELLECTUAL	Senses/ Perception				●	
	Concepts/ Vocabulary					
	School Skills					

DIFFICULTY LEVELS

Other Areas: Sensory Experiences

Specific Value

From babyhood onward, children have always enjoyed the jingle of keys and the magic around how keys open up special places. This large board of assorted keys provides a great deal of practice in skills of physical coordination, but it also presents some challenging tasks. Children can look for similar details on the keys, can compare sizes and can use their imaginations about how keys are a part of stories and their own lives. It is an open-ended activity, loaded with success and good feeling, yet children can add challenges such as varied configurations of keys and sizes.

Child's Readiness

If the child can use small hooks and rings then he or she is ready to participate in this activity. There will be lots of interest when children enjoy being persistent, like to sort, and like to discuss imaginative ideas concerning keys, surprises, etc.

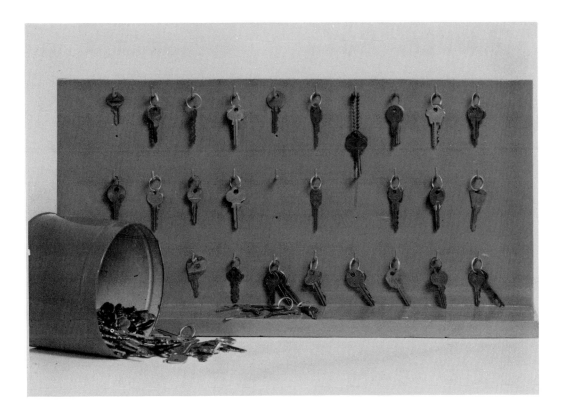

Applications

Any young child will love using real keys; they are interesting to see, hear and feel. Handicapped children can practice their physical skills with these delightful key rings.

Variations and Related Ideas

Although keys do have a special appeal here, other materials can be used such as loops, chain segments, hardware, buttons, etc. Matching games where children identify like keys, and serial games can be played (which comes first). You can make up a variety of stories around keys. Children can trace them to study their shapes, keeping within their outlines, and create matching games.

Comments

At last you found a useful purpose for your old keys! Everyone you know has at least a few. You can add to the learning for the child in many ways, but the fun of this activity is still in the child's own type of participation.

13 WHEEL BOX

AREA

Physical: Gross Motor

PURPOSE

To explore uses of the hand and arms to produce an effect.

Place in Development

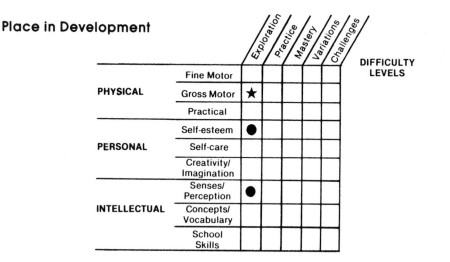

		Exploration	Practice	Mastery	Variations	Challenges	DIFFICULTY LEVELS
PHYSICAL	Fine Motor						
	Gross Motor	★					
	Practical						
PERSONAL	Self-esteem	●					
	Self-care						
	Creativity/ Imagination						
INTELLECTUAL	Senses/ Perception	●					
	Concepts/ Vocabulary						
	School Skills						

Other Areas: Self-esteem

Specific Value

Children who are in the early stages of developing physical coordination skills are often involved in tasks that challenge them. Here is an activity that is designed to produce a large, satisfying effect in a safely contained space, easily. It is very sturdy and can be used repeatedly. The texture and natural appeal of the wheels provide extra motivation to try and to persist in making an effect.

Child's Readiness

The Wheel Box is especially appropriate for children with minimal or beginning physical skills. They can simply swipe at the wheel with a broad arm stroke.

Applications

Toddlers are simply unable to resist batting these wheels and watching them turn. Severely handicapped children will enjoy this simple but very enjoyable activity.

Variations and Related Ideas

Because they are large, these wheels are valuable in this particular set of materials. Yet, any other objects with suitable centers (for the axle) could be used. A good-sized abacus might be attempted later, since the same swing style of arm action is needed to produce the effect. Painted balls might be very attractive for a color swirl, an interesting variation.

Comments

You may be able to use bicycle grease to keep the wheel turning freely.

14 BUCKET BALL

AREA

Physical: Gross Motor

PURPOSE

To explore a gross motor coordination task.

Place in Development

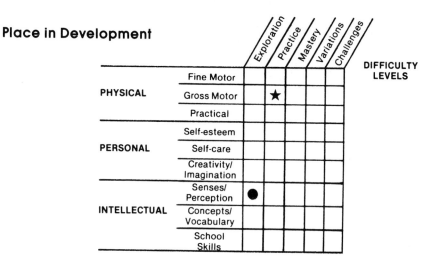

		Exploration	Practice	Mastery	Variations	Challenges
PHYSICAL	Fine Motor					
	Gross Motor	★				
	Practical					
PERSONAL	Self-esteem					
	Self-care					
	Creativity/ Imagination					
INTELLECTUAL	Senses/ Perception	●				
	Concepts/ Vocabulary					
	School Skills					

DIFFICULTY LEVELS

Other Areas: Intellectual

Specific Value

Children love making objects disappear inside containers. This soft and manageable version of basketball will build their ability to negotiate hand and arm movements at the same time that it serves to delight them. The child also has to empty the balls inside to repeat the task; they thereby learn a useful sequence of activities. The simple structure or rule here is another kind of learning—that of aiming to place the ball inside without it falling or bouncing out.

Child's Readiness

This activity is a relatively easy one, yet an appropriate challenge for youngsters with the interest and ability to succeed some of the time.

Applications

Toddlers may even attempt to "throw" the ball into the bucket.
The physically handicapped child who shows few coordination skills will want to try
this activity.

Variations and Related Ideas

Once children enjoy simply placing the soft balls into the bucket they can play a
game that requires selecting a ball of a specific color or they can learn to remember
what is underneath the upturned bucket. There is also the possibility of laying the
container on its side and rolling the ball into it. A group ball game might even be attempted with an adult and another child.

Comments

The soft, easy-to-grab balls will make the child's participation especially enjoyable
here.

15 CHIME AND BELL BOXES

AREA

Physical: Gross Motor

PURPOSE

To practice swiping at responsive materials.

Place in Development

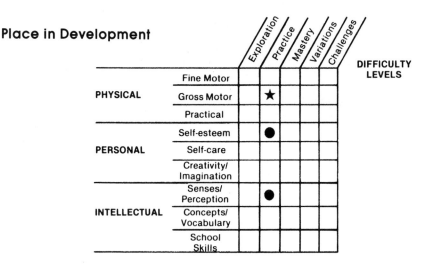

		Exploration	Practice	Mastery	Variations	Challenges	DIFFICULTY LEVELS
PHYSICAL	Fine Motor						
	Gross Motor	★					
	Practical						
PERSONAL	Self-esteem	●					
	Self-care						
	Creativity/ Imagination						
INTELLECTUAL	Senses/ Perception	●					
	Concepts/ Vocabulary						
	School Skills						

Other Areas: Self-esteem; Sensory Stimulation

Specific Value

Chimes and bells are made for movement, with wind or hands used to bring about pleasant sounds. In these materials, the child is clearly invited to use arms and hands to succeed in producing an effect. The chimes and bells respond immediately, to the delight of the children and even with the approval of adults who appreciate the musical result. It's good exercise and satisfying to everyone. It can be repeated. The visual swaying effect is likewise a pleasant and reinforcing one for the child. The materials are sturdy and secure enough to withstand even vigorous or uncoordinated swipes.

Child's Readiness

Any very young or handicapped child can participate happily and successfully with the Chime and Bell Boxes.

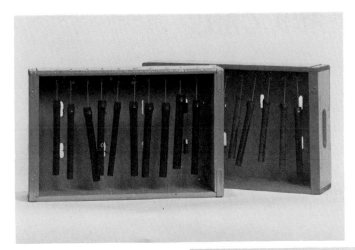

Applications

Toddlers will be regularly attracted to these; so will preschoolers interested in music. Severely handicapped and autistic children may particularly enjoy the musical boxes.

Variations and Related Ideas

Musical instruments of several varieties can be used in ways similar to those of the Chime and Bell Boxes, if they are securely anchored. Since sound effects vary, it is possible to create games where the child can identify the cause and location of a sound. Musical activities can include these boxes. In addition to chimes and bells, shells, metal washers, and other items can be used successfully.

Comments

Short strings and a secure hook and knots will ensure a sturdy material with a minimum of tangling when used.

16 BASKETS AND CANS

AREA

Physical: Gross Motor

PURPOSE

To practice placing large objects into a large space.

Place in Development

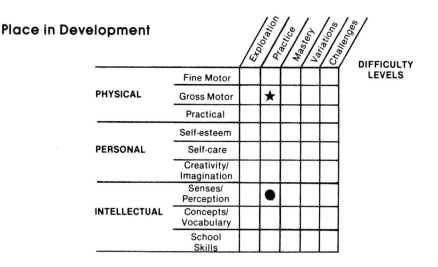

		Exploration	Practice	Mastery	Variations	Challenges	DIFFICULTY LEVELS
PHYSICAL	Fine Motor						
	Gross Motor	★					
	Practical						
PERSONAL	Self-esteem						
	Self-care						
	Creativity/ Imagination						
INTELLECTUAL	Senses/ Perception	●					
	Concepts/ Vocabulary						
	School Skills						

Other Areas: Sensory Stimulation

Specific Value

The successful placement of interesting objects into containers is a satisfying activity for children with beginning motor abilities in this area. Their observations of this achievement and their independence in obtaining it contribute to their motivation to keep trying. Arm and hand coordination can thus be enhanced. The cans are particularly appealing to the children because they clatter so delightfully!

Child's Readiness

The large cans and generously sized containers make this activity appropriate early in the child's development. They can enjoy themselves and be successful even within their limitations.

Applications

Little ones will take out and put in these cans over and over again.
The physically handicapped child should love this made-for-success activity.

Variations and Related Ideas

Try any interesting, unbreakable containers or objects. The children will love plastic and wood materials. Giant pine cones are also quite wonderful. With all of these objects, you can count them, stack them, line them up, and bang them. You can compare the lettering or the dents. You can touch and rub the smooth, bumpy, and shiny surfaces. You can talk about all these treats to the senses.

Comments

Be sure to secure all of the rough edges with tape or glue. You might want to also discourage throwing or knocking down the cans before the children give it a try!

17 THE DROPPING BOX
Caps and Nuts

AREA

Physical: Gross Motor

PURPOSE

To master directed reaching and releasing using arms and hands.

Place in Development

		Exploration	Practice	Mastery	Variations	Challenges	
PHYSICAL	Fine Motor			●			DIFFICULTY LEVELS
	Gross Motor			★			
	Practical						
PERSONAL	Self-esteem						
	Self-care						
	Creativity/ Imagination						
INTELLECTUAL	Senses/ Perception			●			
	Concepts/ Vocabulary		●				
	School Skills						

Other Areas: Fine Motor; Sensory Experiences

Specific Value

Popping objects through a hole and hearing the resulting noise is a highly satisfying experience. In this activity children can use their whole hands (fingers, too, if they are able) to scoop up bottle tops and nuts and bring them to the wide opening in the box and release them. Because they are using sets of objects, they can repeat this physical skill over and over again without becoming saturated too quickly. They will also want to examine them and bring in similar materials from home.

Child's Readiness

Most youngsters will be able to negotiate this activity even though it requires some fine motor as well as gross motor skill and some coordination.

Applications

Older toddlers love this type of activity once they are past the mouthing stage. Children confined to chairs will delight in seeing and hearing these objects. So will a blind child!

Variations and Related Ideas

Once again, counting and studying objects is part of the appeal of this activity. It will be especially enjoyable if the particular objects are changed every week. Be sure you select something that makes a good noise when it hits bottom! For a small group activity you might try incorporating some adding operations as well as nature study that closely examines the qualities of the objects.

Comments

Very young children will want to use these materials, but the small size of the caps and nuts creates a safety hazard for them.

18 DISPLAY TRAYS
Silverware, Buttons, and Pennies

AREA

Physical: Gross Motor and Fine Motor

PURPOSE

To handle and organize familiar objects.

Place in Development

		Exploration	Practice	Mastery	Variations	Challenges	
							DIFFICULTY LEVELS
PHYSICAL	Fine Motor				●		
	Gross Motor				★		
	Practical						
PERSONAL	Self-esteem						
	Self-care						
	Creativity/ Imagination		●				
INTELLECTUAL	Senses/ Perception		●				
	Concepts/ Vocabulary		●				
	School Skills						

Other Areas: Sensory Experiences; Creativity

Specific Value

The opportunity to handle real objects is something all children enjoy and something that has the potential for learning through exploration. These Display Trays permit children to touch and feel real things. They can use their own judgment as well in deciding how to arrange them in the open and partitioned trays. Larger objects will help develop gross motor skills whereas the smaller items encourage fine motor development. The sorting operations also stimulate the intellect by highlighting the qualities by which objects can be categorized.

Child's Readiness

Children will need to have some ability to use their hands in order to find this activity satisfying. The buttons and pennies are a bit more difficult to pick up.

Applications

Preschoolers should relate to these arrays quite enjoyably because of their interest in sets of objects.

The Display Trays are very appropriate lap and table activities for the handicapped youngster.

Variations and Related Ideas

Any interesting materials can be used here. Familiar ones are particularly inviting for children. The child who seems interested can also deal with amounts, sizes and colors while sorting. Vocabulary and concepts might be included in conjunction with the variety of materials used. Children may want to trace the materials for an art project or use them with Play-Doh.

Comments

It might be very helpful for children if there are always larger and smaller items because each will challenge different muscle groups.

19 SORT AND HANG
Mittens, Socks, and Cloths

AREA

Physical: Gross Motor

PURPOSE

To practice hanging up, sorting, and arranging familiar and colorful mitten pairs on a rack.

Place in Development

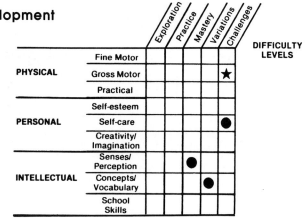

		Exploration	Practice	Mastery	Variations	Challenges	
							DIFFICULTY LEVELS
PHYSICAL	Fine Motor						
	Gross Motor				★		
	Practical						
PERSONAL	Self-esteem						
	Self-care				●		
	Creativity/ Imagination						
INTELLECTUAL	Senses/ Perception		●				
	Concepts/ Vocabulary			●			
	School Skills						

Other Areas: Intellectual; Concepts

Specific Value

Activities that invite children to organize and sort materials involve both the intellect and many physical skills. Hanging up objects demands the coordination of several muscle groups. Deciding which mitten to place where, how to pair them, how to line them up to be visually interesting—these activities make use of children's thinking skills as well. Notions of color, pairing, and right and left are developed.

Real mittens and socks are delightful for children to handle and sort. They help the child to develop pride in the practical area of taking care of one's own belongings. The satisfaction of seeing small garments neatly hanging up can provoke interest in caring for other garments—sweaters, coats, towels, for example.

Child's Readiness

Once the child is able to hang large rings or loops onto large hooks, he or she will want to try smaller hooks such as are provided here. Interest in useful practical skills can also serve as motivation.

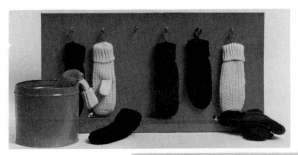

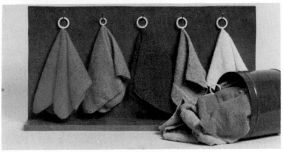

Applications

Young preschoolers will immediately want to try this activity, varying the arrangement of colors to mix and match according to their fancy.

Retarded children will particularly enjoy the mastery of this practical skill. They may want loops on their own mittens.

Variations and Related Ideas

Many objects can be used besides mittens, socks and cloths. Children can use assorted gloves and mittens from family members and classmates—remembering the owners' names! Games of "whose are whose" can be delightful! Learning can be extended by helping children to talk about colors, shapes, other clothing, care, and ownership.

Comments

Parents and teachers should permit the child free and open access to this exploring activity. The mittens and loops may need washing and mending from time to time.

20 DOOR OPENER

AREA

Physical: Practical

PURPOSE

To explore and practice the skills needed to use a door knob.

Place in Development

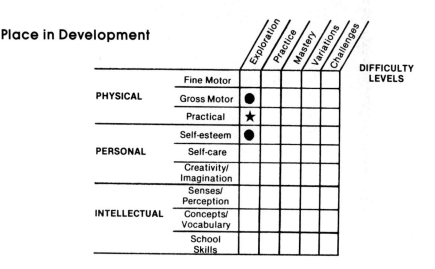

DIFFICULTY LEVELS

		Exploration	Practice	Mastery	Variations	Challenges
	Fine Motor					
PHYSICAL	Gross Motor	●				
	Practical	★				
	Self-esteem	●				
PERSONAL	Self-care					
	Creativity/ Imagination					
	Senses/ Perception					
INTELLECTUAL	Concepts/ Vocabulary					
	School Skills					

Other Areas: Self-esteem

Specific Value

To young and handicapped children, learning how to open a closed door is often a formidable task. There are a series of motor coordinations needed to bring about success, i.e., turning the knob, pulling the door open, swinging it on its hinges. The development of this skill is important to children because it is required throughout their daily experiences. The opportunity to practice it (on a slightly more manageable scale) not only makes them more capable, but adds to their positive views of themselves as successful.

Child's Readiness

The Door Opener is appropriate for children with beginning gross- and fine-motor skills.

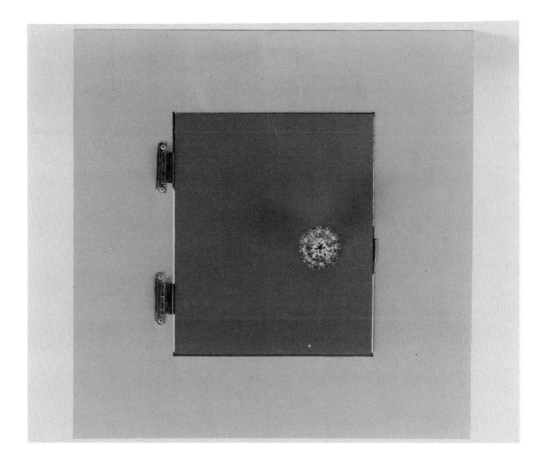

Applications

Toddlers delight in opening and closing cabinets and this is quite similar.
Very handicapped children will love this realistic challenge.

Variations and Related Ideas

Peek-a-boo and hidden objects games can be added to this activity. Remembering
what is behind the door requires some attention and thinking; different pictures can
be easily inserted inside and adults can then organize some of the children's ques-
tioning.

Comments

Use an interesting doorknob—it adds to the fun!

21 DOORBELL

AREA

Physical: Practical

PURPOSE

To explore the components and effects of pressing a doorbell.

Place in Development

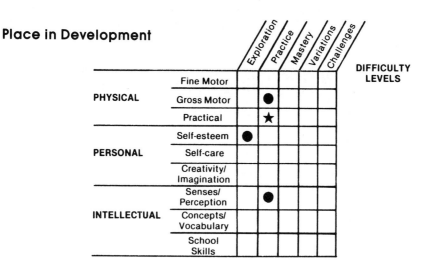

		Exploration	Practice	Mastery	Variations	Challenges	DIFFICULTY LEVELS
PHYSICAL	Fine Motor						
	Gross Motor		●				
	Practical		★				
PERSONAL	Self-esteem	●					
	Self-care						
	Creativity/ Imagination						
INTELLECTUAL	Senses/ Perception		●				
	Concepts/ Vocabulary						
	School Skills						

Other Areas: Intellectual; Concepts

Specific Value

What a joy it is for children to really ring a doorbell! How much better when it's mounted on a board for close examination. The child learns not only the practical skill of obtaining the needed sound, but gains in understanding about the bell that is sounded as a result of pressing the button.

Child's Readiness

This is a delightfully easy, early task that will continue to fascinate the children across several levels of ability.

Applications

Throughout the preschool age range, children will delight in this doorbell.
Blind children and those with other physical restrictions can still manage and enjoy
    this activity.

Variations and Related Ideas

The possibilities for interesting dramatic or pretend play with a real doorbell are
endless. Children will want to take turns pretending to enter and leave homes, prob-
ably in various stages of dressing, carrying suitcases and purses, using shoes or
boots, etc.

Comments

Certainly batteries are safer to use here than an electrical cord and plug, but expect
to renew the batteries because the children will use them frequently.

22 LIGHT SWITCHES

AREA

Physical: Practical

PURPOSE

To explore and practice two ways of turning on a light.

Place in Development

		Exploration	Practice	Mastery	Variations	Challenges	DIFFICULTY LEVELS
PHYSICAL	Fine Motor	●					
	Gross Motor						
	Practical		★				
PERSONAL	Self-esteem	●					
	Self-care						
	Creativity/ Imagination						
INTELLECTUAL	Senses/ Perception	●					
	Concepts/ Vocabulary		●				
	School Skills						

Other Areas: Intellectual; Concepts

Specific Value

Most young and handicapped children are not permitted to turn lights on and off by themselves. It is considered a risk to them as well as very inconvenient to adults. This is an activity that cannot be duplicated easily except in the school situation. The Light Switches provide the opportunity to rehearse physical skills and stimulate thinking about how things work.

Child's Readiness

Because glass lightbulbs are needed here the activity requires both supervision from adults and/or some awareness of safety rules in the children.

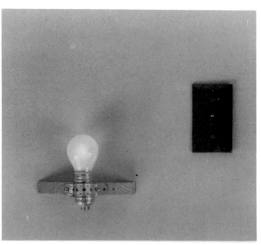

Applications

Older preschoolers will want to study this project at length.
Retarded children or those with many physical handicaps will find this highly satisfying.

Variations and Related Ideas

Light switches can be practiced not only for the development of physical skills but
also in relation to beginning science activities. For the less capable child, the
materials can be a source of a delightful sense of mastery of some part of the world
around them. For fun, try varying the light bulb color, shape, and brightness!

Comments

Be careful of damp fingers on light switches and caution children about the heat of
the bulb. Perhaps a simple shade will prevent contact.

23 SHOE SHOP

AREA

Physical: Practical

PURPOSE

To develop sorting skills and a sense of caring for one's belongings.

Place in Development

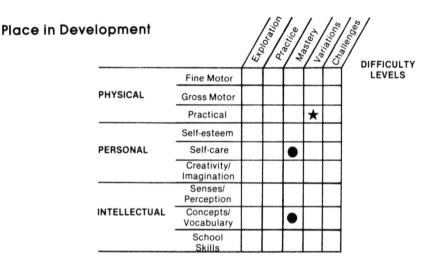

		Exploration	Practice	Mastery	Variations	Challenges	
							DIFFICULTY LEVELS
PHYSICAL	Fine Motor						
	Gross Motor						
	Practical				★		
PERSONAL	Self-esteem						
	Self-care		●				
	Creativity/ Imagination						
INTELLECTUAL	Senses/ Perception						
	Concepts/ Vocabulary		●				
	School Skills						

Other Areas: Vocabulary; Concepts

Specific Value

Real shoes are provocative. They stimulate a great deal of discussion about their who's, what's, and where's. They insist on being matched together in pairs. If they vary greatly in size and style, they are assumed to belong to persons of corresponding ages and occupations. An old shoe has a history as well, undoubtedly interesting if you use your imagination.

Child's Readiness

While even the very inexperienced child could sort and match the shoes, those with some verbal skills could exercise their abilities to create some lively discussion.

Applications

Very young children may wish to try these on—that's fine!
These shoes may even stimulate some interest from a very withdrawn child or a burst
of utterances from a language delayed child.

Variations and Related Ideas

The particular shoes used here can reflect growth, i.e., babies to older children, or occupations (work boots, nurses' shoes), or weather and seasons (boots, sandles).
Adult shoes can be added to dramatic play. Rubber family and helper figures can be
matched to shoes, or photographs of children can be used with the actual, saved
shoes. In all of these activities there is a good deal of learning of many kinds.

Comments

Don't worry about the scuffs and marks on shoes—that is part of their special appeal!

24 TABLE SETTING

AREA

Physical: Practical

PURPOSE

To use physical skills for a practical activity.

Place in Development

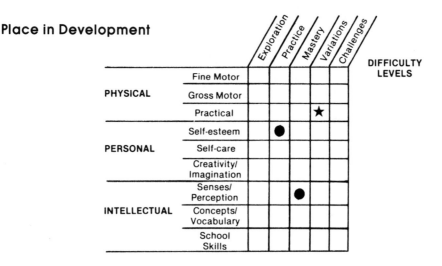

DIFFICULTY LEVELS

		Exploration	Practice	Mastery	Variations	Challenges
PHYSICAL	Fine Motor					
	Gross Motor					
	Practical			★		
PERSONAL	Self-esteem	●				
	Self-care					
	Creativity/ Imagination					
INTELLECTUAL	Senses/ Perception		●			
	Concepts/ Vocabulary					
	School Skills					

Other Areas: School Skills; Perception

Specific Value

The ability to organize one arrangement of materials so that they match another has both physical and intellectual components. It means the child can perceive discrepancies between the two, if incorrectly matched, and can understand how to bring them into correspondence with one another. To practice and succeed with a meaningful, practical task such as arranging a table setting is particularly valuable.

Child's Readiness

This task is moderately challenging and enjoyable for those children who are interested in accurately duplicating this array.

Applications

Kindergartners can appreciate the many dramatic play possibilities here. Retarded children will be able to use and enjoy this applied skill.

Variations and Related Ideas

Table setting can also be practiced in the playhouse or pretend role-play area of the program. Once children are comfortable with the task, why not add some spice to it—a candle, salt and pepper shakers, glasses, a vase of flowers, or a tablecloth? Children can even learn the names and purposes of various glassware.

Comments

It's important to use real dishes and silverware here, but do rely on unbreakables as well.

25 DOOR AND KEY LATCHES

AREA

Physical: Practical

PURPOSE

To apply motor skills to different locking mechanisms.

Place in Development

		Exploration	Practice	Mastery	Variations	Challenges	DIFFICULTY LEVELS
PHYSICAL	Fine Motor					●	
	Gross Motor					●	
	Practical				★		
PERSONAL	Self-esteem						
	Self-care						
	Creativity/ Imagination						
INTELLECTUAL	Senses/ Perception						
	Concepts/ Vocabulary		●				
	School Skills						

Other Areas: Intellectual

Specific Value

Door locks represent a not uncommon challenge to children in their daily environments. While they may not be called upon to regularly use a lock, it certainly helps if they are capable of doing so when it becomes necessary. The latches used here are real, with the sturdy quality of the genuine article. The child who masters these materials will have developed physical and intellectual skills in the fine and gross motor areas. What's more, he or she will feel a part of the capable adult world when these skills are established.

Child's Readiness

To prevent frustration this activity is most appropriate for the somewhat capable youngster who enjoys the challenge.

Applications

Older preschoolers can be expected to repeat their successes many times over just to handle the materials.

Retarded children will love the "I can do it" feeling of this practical activity.

Variations and Related Ideas

Slide bolt locks and pin locks might be added here. The padlock door can also be used with a variety of key and combination locks. As with the Door Opener, photos and pictures might be used inside the actual door. More than one lock can be used for more advanced children.

Comments

You'll need to keep an extra key handy in case one gets lost!

26 TELEPHONE DIAL

AREA

Physical: Practical

PURPOSE

To try the complicated task of dealing with dials and numbers in a sequence.

Place in Development

		Exploration	Practice	Mastery	Variations	Challenges
PHYSICAL	Fine Motor					●
	Gross Motor					
	Practical					★
PERSONAL	Self-esteem					
	Self-care					
	Creativity/ Imagination					
INTELLECTUAL	Senses/ Perception					
	Concepts/ Vocabulary				●	●
	School Skills					

DIFFICULTY LEVELS

Other Areas: Intellectual; Vocabulary

Specific Value

How wonderful to be able to practice dialing one's own phone number! It is an extremely valuable practical skill that requires a good deal of repetition as well as memory skills. The telephone is also a natural stimulant for extending conversation skills. You must talk when you telephone. For this activity the dialing process is the focus for learning to apply numbers in a sequence and use the dial in a systematic way. To ease the memory requirements the number is clearly presented.

Child's Readiness

Because of its complexity and the blend of intellectual and physical skills, this activity should be considered to be at the advanced level.

Applications

A perfect kindergarten task!
This is a comfortable long-range learning task even for blind and retarded children.

Variations and Related Ideas

Emergency call numbers can also be practiced here, to the child's benefit as well as to others. Children might do a bit of homework as well, if parents can find understanding relatives and operators! Telephone lists can be posted and practiced at more advanced stages. Don't forget to encourage children to learn telephone manners as well—from hellos to relaying messages.

Comments

Most phone companies will applaud the conscientious teacher who wishes to help children dial properly—they will likely donate one on request.

27 BIKE LOCK

AREA

Physical: Practical

PURPOSE

To try applying physical and mental skills to practical needs.

Place in Development

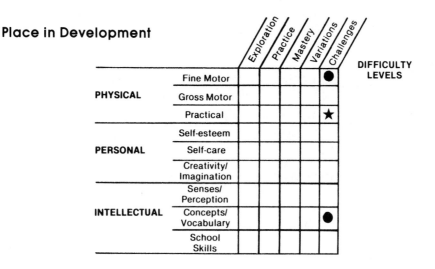

		Exploration	Practice	Mastery	Variations	Challenges	DIFFICULTY LEVELS
PHYSICAL	Fine Motor					●	
	Gross Motor						
	Practical					★	
PERSONAL	Self-esteem						
	Self-care						
	Creativity/ Imagination						
INTELLECTUAL	Senses/ Perception						
	Concepts/ Vocabulary					●	
	School Skills						

Other Areas: Intellectual

Specific Value

Whether you ride a tricycle or sit on a rocking horse, there is something appealing about having and using your own bike lock. That's what this material implies even though the major focus is deciphering how to undo the combination lock. The physical skills are nested with the intellectual here even though the critical numbers are clearly presented. Lots of practice with a good bit of concentration will undoubtedly be seen, as the child's motivation is typically quite strong for this activity.

Child's Readiness

This is a fun activity, but nonetheless a challenging one for most children.

Applications

Kindergarten children can practice this rather complicated task with some success. The confined child will love this touch of real world that might not otherwise be available.

Variations and Related Ideas

Why not really put this on a wheel to take on and off as a reward for succeeding with the lock? It certainly would promote lots of study and work to succeed. There are several other styles of bike locks and chains on the market as well. Perhaps parents will want to let the child practice at home. (The different combination would certainly challenge the thinking of any child as to the workings of locks.)

Comments

It is rather difficult to remember the reversal of direction here; you may want to create a musical tune with the numbers and two "about-face" phrases.

II. PERSONAL AREA OF DEVELOPMENT

A child's personal and social growth is at once the most pervasive but also the most elusive area of development to focus on or to work with. Personal skills provide a base for other learning activities. The confident, secure, and curious child is able to concentrate and persist in learning even when challenges seem overwhelming. The child's affective development thus influences success, but is also created from it. The more you succeed, the better you feel. Adults often overlook this vital area of growth. Curriculum guides seldom include suggestions for building the esteem and confidence needed to learn more. The activities (28 to 47) in this area are thus designed to focus primarily on enhancing this personal growth.

Self-esteem and self-concept are one aspect of this growth. These are the terms often used to describe the good feelings in people, the sense of "I'm OK." Esteem comes partly from getting to know oneself better and also from having others relate to one as a special, individual person. Self-care is the second aspect of personal growth and it is a bit more familiar. The process of caring for one's clothing and belongings is a way of approaching the child's development of self and personal respect. The third aspect is creativity or the expression of one's own ideas. Creative ideas are valuable in education and development because they provide a window from personal feelings and notions to the social world beyond oneself. They enhance communication and bring people and their environments closer.

PERSONAL AREA OF DEVELOPMENT

Aspects of Personal Growth

Levels of difficulty	Self-esteem (I'm OK)	Self-care (my care of me)	Creativity (my own ideas)
Exploration (getting ac- quainted with the materials)	28 / Me in the Mirror	35 / Zippers to Zip 36 / Fur and Buckles	43 / Felt Drawing
Practice (experimenting and trying)	29 / Right Hand– Left Hand 30 / Body Board	37 / Cup Hanging 38 / Belts and Buckles	44 / Nail Drawing
Mastery (succeeding)	31 / My Health Book	39 / Bunches of Buttons	45 / Threading Around
Variations (trying other ideas)	32 / Lining Up My Name	40 / Close It Up: Grippers and Hooks	46 / Wire Weaving
Advanced skills (complex challenges)	33 / Writing my Name 34 / Writing My Phone Number	41 / Lacing Vest 42 / Shoe Tying	47 / Hole Drawing

28 ME IN THE MIRROR

AREA

Personal: Self-esteem

PURPOSE

To look at one's image and explore facial features.

Place in Development

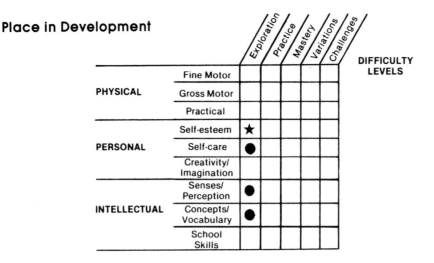

		Exploration	Practice	Mastery	Variations	Challenges	DIFFICULTY LEVELS
PHYSICAL	Fine Motor						
	Gross Motor						
	Practical						
PERSONAL	Self-esteem	★					
	Self-care	●					
	Creativity/ Imagination						
INTELLECTUAL	Senses/ Perception	●					
	Concepts/ Vocabulary	●					
	School Skills						

Other Areas: Vocabulary; Self-care and Grooming

Specific Value

Children's concepts about themselves are largely shaped by the experiences they have, both with other people and in their own ability to succeed or fail. Their views of themselves also need to be based on what they see. Mirrors help children study themselves on their own terms. They can quietly look at their bodies and faces, perhaps even experiment with acting out facial expressions such as smiles or grimaces. They gain a better sense of themselves as well as experience pleasure in reflections whose movements and gestures match their own.

Child's Readiness

Children at all ages and stages can enjoy looking at mirrors, although glass should be used only when there is no risk of banging or dropping.

Applications

Toddlers and preschoolers greatly enjoy using mirrors of all sizes and shapes, sometimes vocalizing and smiling into them.

A deaf child can learn a great deal about mouth movements from observing himself or herself in the mirror.

Variations and Related Ideas

Mirrors come in several sizes and types so it is easy to mix two or three on a board. A magnifying mirror is a great curiosity to children. Full-length and three-way mirrors would be especially valuable in studying oneself.

Comments

Whenever possible, unbreakable mirrors are preferable so that the chance of injury is reduced. Remember also that mirrors reverse images. Some children can experiment with deciphering backwards messages!

29 RIGHT HAND-LEFT HAND

AREA

Personal: Self-esteem

PURPOSE

To practice distinguishing right and left hands and placing mittens on the corresponding hands.

Place in Development

		Exploration	Practice	Mastery	Variations	Challenges	DIFFICULTY LEVELS
PHYSICAL	Fine Motor	●	●				
	Gross Motor	●	●				
	Practical						
PERSONAL	Self-esteem		★				
	Self-care		●				
	Creativity/ Imagination						
INTELLECTUAL	Senses/ Perception		●				
	Concepts/ Vocabulary						
	School Skills						

Other Areas: Motor Development and Perception

Specific Value

Understanding right and left is an important concern in the early years, but especially when it applies to one's own body. Children's self-awareness is built up from information they gain, such as the names of their body parts. The concept of right and left is a personal one because so much clothing as well as many activities require knowing about these directions. Children typically feel very good about mastering this personal concept.

Child's Readiness

This material can be used on several levels, but it is most helpful when the child can match mitten to hand and use words to explain right and left. Some physical dexterity is also needed.

Applications

The young preschooler who struggles with his or her own mittens will love applying
the skill to this material.

Retarded children may enjoy rehearsing these skills and using labels with this
material.

Variations and Related Ideas

What better variation for this material than to mix up mitten styles and colors and try
gloves! Children will also want to match up their hands and fingers. They might try
tracing their friends' hands and comparing them with the wooden hands. At more
advanced stages the children can gain from the use of the printed words right and
left. They can try them out with shoes as well.

Comments

At first, children may have difficulty with the thumb, just as they do on their own mittens. It will help if oversized mittens are used.

30 BODY BOARD

AREA

Personal: Self-esteem

PURPOSE

To explore body parts and gestures.

Place in Development

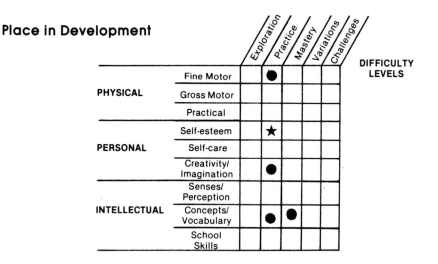

Other Areas: Vocabulary and Concepts; Creativity

Specific Value

To young and old alike, the body is a fascinating thing. There is a great deal to learn and understand about its parts—how they move and what they do. The mannequin on the Body Board will demonstrate a variety of actions and give the child the sense of a complete, connected figure resembling his or her own body. The sense of self that children gain from examining and talking about bodies is as important as the specific words they also learn.

Child's Readiness

After some time is spent in simple exploration, children who are able to respond to words and positions can practice movements and compare the mannequin to their own bodies.

Applications

Most children will enjoy the unusual and fascinating moveable body.
Blind children might appreciate feeling this body and the movements that can be
changed.

Variations and Related Ideas

Once children are able to think in terms of body parts and movements, they may try
games like "Simon Says" where gestures are copied by the mannequin according to
the children's requests. A flashlight can also be used to create shadow gestures. The
mannequin might be dressed up and compared to a doll-type action figure such as
those children have at home. Conversation about these figures is usually full of ideas
that can be shared among friends.

Comments

The mannequin on the Body Board needs to be firmly fastened to withstand the
children's manipulations.

31 MY HEALTH BOOK

AREA

Personal: Self-esteem

PURPOSE

To understand basic health concepts and to feel good about applying them to oneself.

Place in Development

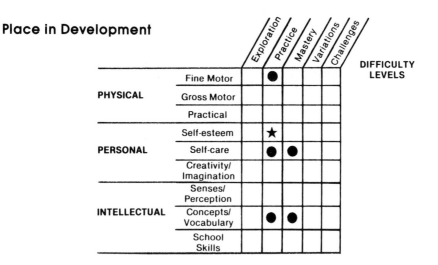

		Exploration	Practice	Mastery	Variations	Challenges
PHYSICAL	Fine Motor	●				
	Gross Motor					
	Practical					
PERSONAL	Self-esteem	★				
	Self-care	●	●			
	Creativity/ Imagination					
INTELLECTUAL	Senses/ Perception					
	Concepts/ Vocabulary	●	●			
	School Skills					

DIFFICULTY LEVELS

Other Areas: Self-care; Physical Growth

Specific Value

Young children often take great pride in obtaining their own personal belongings and using them in practical ways. Such activities make them feel grown-up and competent. My Health Book is designed to build the child's sense of mastery over these understandings, without requiring them to fully master the use of the materials involved. They can examine and explore them freely while also developing ideas and recognizing the value of health care.

Child's Readiness

My Health Book can be used with children at many different levels of understanding. Some concepts such as specific uses, labels, and schedules of care will occur at more advanced levels.

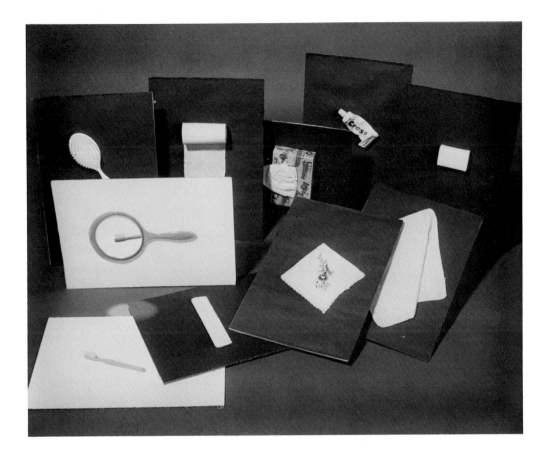

Applications

Most children will take great pleasure in sorting through this collection of real and related objects.

Retarded children can gradually build their understanding of self-care with these materials.

Variations and Related Ideas

Some children will really want to employ these items. They can be kept in a box to use with dolls during children's dramatic playtime. Children can also create their own individual sets of health items at home and at school. Parents appreciate such school support for activities they encourage at home. Picture books (of the two-dimensional sort) will reinforce these concepts, as will posters and demonstrations by nurses or physicians.

Comments

Some children may have a difficult time refraining from pulling out the tissues or rubbing the washcloth in My Health Book. That's a good time to give them their own set!

32 LINING UP MY NAME

AREA

Personal: Self-esteem

PURPOSE

To begin to deal with words and letters in a personal and important way for the child—his or her own name!

Place in Development

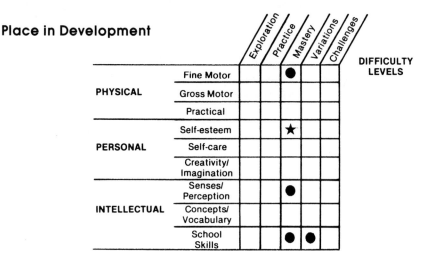

		Exploration	Practice	Mastery	Variations	Challenges	
PHYSICAL	Fine Motor			●			**DIFFICULTY LEVELS**
	Gross Motor						
	Practical						
PERSONAL	Self-esteem		★				
	Self-care						
	Creativity/ Imagination						
INTELLECTUAL	Senses/ Perception			●			
	Concepts/ Vocabulary						
	School Skills			●	●		

Other Areas: Intellectual: Basic Skills

Specific Value

Nothing is quite as valuable in beginning reading and writing as working with what the child finds important. One's own name is important—how it looks, what letters are in it—yet we cannot expect mastery right away. If the child can use his or her letters to line up the name, it makes the task pleasurable and satisfying, especially when eye-hand coordination is not yet developed enough for writing the letters out by oneself.

It is also important for children to understand that letters have to be in a particular order to be read. This activity will help to build that understanding.

Child's Readiness

The child is ready when he or she wants to know how to make names and can identify the names some of the time, such as when they are on drawings or in a clothing cubby.

Applications

Most children will soon understand the letter order of their name and enjoy practicing this line-up activity.

Retarded children and deaf children will be able to build skills gradually in sounding out the letters that make up their names.

Variations and Related Ideas

After the child can line up his or her own name, then parents', teachers', and friends' names can be used. A model might be needed at first to reproduce the names accurately. Tracing can be used later when the child has mastered the name fully.

Comments

Lots of adult reinforcement and gentle correction will keep the child on target here.

33 WRITING MY NAME

AREA

Personal: Self-esteem

PURPOSE

To apply beginning writing skills to expressing one's personal name.

Place in Development

		Exploration	Practice	Mastery	Variations	Challenges
PHYSICAL	Fine Motor				●	●
	Gross Motor					
	Practical				●	
PERSONAL	Self-esteem				★	
	Self-care					
	Creativity/ Imagination					
INTELLECTUAL	Senses/ Perception			●	●	
	Concepts/ Vocabulary					
	School Skills				●	

DIFFICULTY LEVELS

Other Areas: Physical: Fine Motor; School Skills

Specific Value

To the developing child, it is a joy to be able to write one's name. It feels good to apply one's still limited ability to this basic and necessary expression of oneself. What's more, it feels even better to do it in a situation where mistakes and erasures are expected. The Writing My Name board is designed to build this ability in a relaxed way with an available, easy-to-follow model. In addition, the disappearing nature of the plastic wipe-off sheet often delights little ones!

Child's Readiness

Children should have a familiarity with letters and be somewhat skilled in using crayons and paper and in creating some simple shapes before they attempt to write their name. Motivation is also important; the child should want to succeed with this task.

Applications

Preschool children will enjoy the opportunity to practice their names repeatedly. Physically handicapped children will appreciate the mistakes-allowed nature of this material.

Variations and Related Ideas

The Writing My Name board can be used to practice additional letters, parents' names, or shapes in different colors. The wipe cloth might be part of a memory game where several shapes or letters are drawn and one wiped away; the child guesses which disappeared. Once there is mastery with the child's name as a model, the prewritten letters can be removed one at a time or all together so that the child's skill extends to writing from memory.

Comments

Be sure to write the child's name consistently, especially when using it in different circumstances with upper or lower case letters.

34 WRITING MY PHONE NUMBER

AREA

Personal: Self-esteem

PURPOSE

To apply beginning number recognition and writing skills to expressing one's personal phone number.

Place in Development

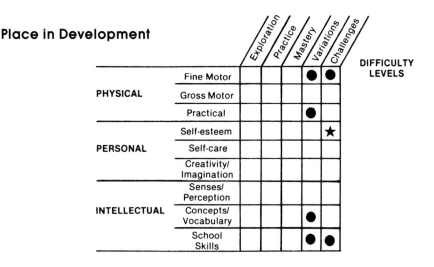

		Exploration	Practice	Mastery	Variations	Challenges	
							DIFFICULTY LEVELS
PHYSICAL	Fine Motor				●	●	
	Gross Motor						
	Practical				●		
PERSONAL	Self-esteem				★		
	Self-care						
	Creativity/ Imagination						
INTELLECTUAL	Senses/ Perception						
	Concepts/ Vocabulary				●		
	School Skills				●	●	

Other Areas: Physical: Fine Motor; Basic Skills

Specific Value

Remembering one's phone number is in some ways more difficult than one's address and much more abstract than one's name. This skill, however, is not only a part of mathematical training, but also a valued way of looking after oneself. A phone number is a complex series of numbers and recognition skills and memory are required. The task is achieved and children will feel secure and connected—if I have any problems I can just call my parents. Do you want to come to visit me on the weekend? Here's my number. It feels good to be able to do these things!

Child's Readiness

The Writing My Phone Number board can be simplified by providing a model of the appropriate numbers. The child, nonetheless, should have the abilities of number recognition, memory, and some writing skills to appreciate this material fully.

Applications

The older preschooler will enjoy practicing this somewhat challenging task.
Older retarded children will greatly value this skill of producing one's phone number.

Variations and Related Ideas

The telephone number used can be varied in a guess-my-number game, or a different series of numbers can be practiced in a memory game. The board may also be enjoyed in the dramatic play or mathematics areas of the children's classroom. Real telephones can be borrowed from the phone company, which can also emphasize emergency call procedures. Parents can be encouraged to reinforce children's learning of their own personal numbers.

Comments

Teachers may need to move slowly in requiring accuracy from children who are still uncertain about phone numbers. The desire for accuracy will ultimately win out over the mistakes!

35 ZIPPERS TO ZIP

AREA

Personal: Self-care

PURPOSE

To explore and practice working zippers similar to those on clothing.

Place in Development

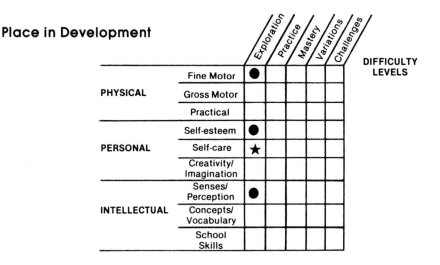

		Exploration	Practice	Mastery	Variations	Challenges	
							DIFFICULTY LEVELS
PHYSICAL	Fine Motor	●					
	Gross Motor						
	Practical						
PERSONAL	Self-esteem	●					
	Self-care	★					
	Creativity/ Imagination						
INTELLECTUAL	Senses/ Perception	●					
	Concepts/ Vocabulary						
	School Skills						

Other Areas: Physical: Fine Motor

Specific Value

Zippers are as much fun as buckles and buttons for children, provided they are able to succeed with them. In this activity, success is built in because the child does not have the added task of bringing two sides of a garment together to start the zipper track. Zippers to Zip is a good beginning along the "I can do it myself" road that children enjoy greatly. It makes self-care less demanding at the earliest stages and prepares the children for applying the skill to their own more difficult clothing later on.

Child's Readiness

Zippers to Zip is an appropriate challenge for children with little skill or ability, yet is also enjoyable for those already able to use zippers on their clothing.

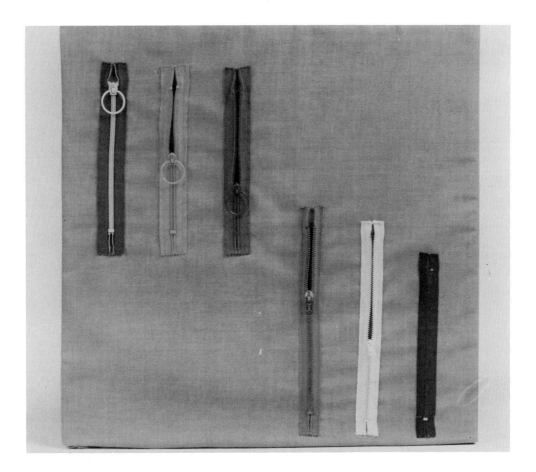

Applications

All children appreciate the simplified nature of these easy-to-use zippers.
Deaf and physically handicapped children will enjoy this colorful and satisfying activity.

Variations and Related Ideas

The particular zippers and fabric used for this material can be varied when it is constructed. Patches of different fabrics for each zipper, for example, would add sensory dimensions to the activity. Sizes and colors can also be varied. Clean, discarded children's garments might be used on the board, as well, to permit practicing on real clothing. These items would most likely employ different types of zippers—an interesting addition to the material.

Comments

Big zipper handles, rings, or even a knot of yarn will make any small zipper head easier to grasp. Silicone spray can free up most sticky zippers.

36 FUR AND BUCKLES

AREA

Personal: Self-care

PURPOSE

To explore and practice how to work buckles on clothing.

Place in Development

		Exploration	Practice	Mastery	Variations	Challenges	
PHYSICAL	Fine Motor	●					**DIFFICULTY LEVELS**
	Gross Motor						
	Practical						
PERSONAL	Self-esteem	●					
	Self-care	★					
	Creativity/ Imagination						
INTELLECTUAL	Senses/ Perception	●					
	Concepts/ Vocabulary						
	School Skills						

Other Areas: Physical: Fine Motor and Eye-hand Coordination

Specific Value

When a child begins to be able to assume some responsibility for the care of personal belongings and dressing, then parents and teachers can begin to provide opportunities to practice some of these skills. Fastening a buckle requires the child to see how the opened edge fits into its companion slot. After fitting these sections together, the child has to remember to press the buckle in a reverse direction to lock. Each step requires coordination. What's more, the child who is successful in fastening his or her clothing feels a personal sense of independence and self-esteem—valuable contributors to further learning. The furry fabric adds a special cuddly feeling much appreciated by little ones!

Child's Readiness

When the child can bring left and right hands together and get them working cooperatively, and when interest in self-care is there, this work board will be used.

Applications

The young preschooler will enjoy practicing with this type of manipulative activity. Touching and rubbing the furry fabric is also a special treat.

A blind older child will be able to use this mounted buckle well because each side is stationary.

Variations and Related Ideas

Other buckles can be used—an old slicker raincoat or a rugged buckled boot, for example, are similar in value. This is also a good time to provide the child with buckled shoes to wear daily!

Comments

Be sure to demonstrate to the child how each part fits into the other. You may need to provide reminders about the final step-locking in a reverse direction. Children will love this added challenge after mastering the initial fitting.

37 CUP HANGING

AREA

Personal: Self-care

PURPOSE

To practice using handles and hooks to hang up beverage cups.

Place in Development

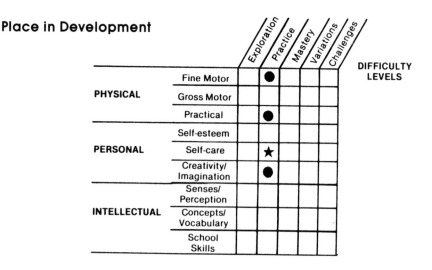

		Exploration	Practice	Mastery	Variations	Challenges	DIFFICULTY LEVELS
PHYSICAL	Fine Motor		●				
	Gross Motor						
	Practical		●				
PERSONAL	Self-esteem						
	Self-care		★				
	Creativity/Imagination		●				
INTELLECTUAL	Senses/Perception						
	Concepts/Vocabulary						
	School Skills						

Other Areas: Physical: Eye-hand Coordination

Specific Value

The practical skill of hanging up personal and household items is one that children need and want to learn. It is often one of the few contributions they can make to family living. The Cup Hanging activity here is a natural, because most children, even the toddler, have their own drinking cups at home. This is also a success-oriented piece of equipment, with simple turned-up hooks and sturdy mug-style cups.

Child's Readiness

Most children can easily manage this task after a little practice, provided they are able to control their arm and hand movements.

Applications

Toddlers will take pride in achieving success here. To them, it will seem *very* grown-up.

Children with cerebral palsy may particularly enjoy the challenge of holding and hooking these cups.

Variations and Related Ideas

The Cup Hanging board can be varied by using different colors and styles of cups, or cups with labels or names on them. These mugs are excellent for playing games where small objects are hidden under cups and the child has to guess the location of each, using attention, concentration, and memory. The board can also be employed in the dramatic play area to store cups used at a small kitchen table.

Comments

Be certain to use unbreakable cups with well-defined handles.

38 BELTS AND BUCKLES

AREA

Personal: Self-care

PURPOSE

To practice using a variety of buckles likely to be found on clothing.

Place in Development

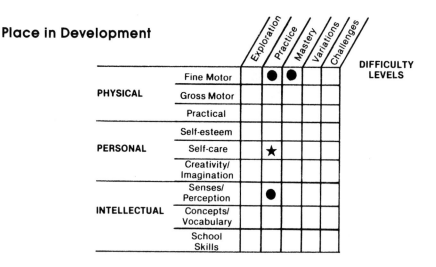

		Exploration	Practice	Mastery	Variations	Challenges	DIFFICULTY LEVELS
PHYSICAL	Fine Motor	●	●				
	Gross Motor						
	Practical						
PERSONAL	Self-esteem						
	Self-care	★					
	Creativity/ Imagination						
INTELLECTUAL	Senses/ Perception	●					
	Concepts/ Vocabulary						
	School Skills						

Other Areas: Physical: Fine Motor

Specific Value

Buckles with a frame and inset piece are somewhat difficult for children to manage, yet these materials are sometimes encountered several times daily. Success in completing a buckle requires a bit of planning as well as physical skill. You have to understand the two-part operation, including the reversal needed to tighten the belt. Belts and Buckles provides a first-step opportunity to gain skill in this activity prior to attempting it on one's own clothing where access is a bit more difficult.

Child's Readiness

Children able to manipulate arms and fingers can begin experimenting with this material. If frustration occurs, try demonstrating the skill several times.

Applications

Older preschoolers interested in dressing themselves will enjoy this activity.
Any handicapped child will appreciate the practice they can get prior to dressing themselves independently.

Variations and Related Ideas

Many kinds of buckles can be placed on the Belts and Buckles board. Old pocket-books may have especially appropriate large buckles. Several shoes could also be placed in a row with varied buckle closures for children to attempt. Children who wear buckled shoes could try out each others' buckles, and an assortment of outgrown belts could also be shared in the group.

Comments

Big buckles are important. Too small a buckle can create frustration. Adults may also need to demonstrate procedures for the children negotiating these materials.

39 BUNCHES OF BUTTONS

AREA

Personal: Self-care

PURPOSE

To master the use of varied button fastenings.

Place in Development

		Exploration	Practice	Mastery	Variations	Challenges
PHYSICAL	Fine Motor			●	●	
	Gross Motor					
	Practical					
PERSONAL	Self-esteem			●		
	Self-care			★		
	Creativity/ Imagination					
INTELLECTUAL	Senses/ Perception			●		
	Concepts/ Vocabulary			●		
	School Skills					

DIFFICULTY LEVELS

Other Areas: Physical: Fine Motor

Specific Value

Buttons are useful for so many different activities, from matching to sorting and counting. Here, four sets of buttons are used for practicing the self-care skill of buttoning one's clothing. For the able or handicapped child, the task of buttoning up can be a formidable one, yet when it is achieved the child becomes independently able to look after dressing himself or herself. This independence is an important developmental task of childhood. Bunches of Buttons can help children work on this skill in a playful way with one's friends or alone.

Child's Readiness

When the child has sufficient physical skills to demonstrate occasional success with buttons, then he or she is ready to use this material.

Applications

Young children will love mastering this activity. They also delight in the visual attractiveness of buttons.

Any handicapped child who strives toward self-dressing will appreciate this practice.

Variations and Related Ideas

The variety of buttons and fabrics is unlimited for Bunches of Buttons. Consistency in color and shape may be important some of the time, but variety is useful for provoking the child's curiosity and desire to talk about the unusual shapes or designs of some buttons. The direction of the button holes can also be varied, as can the type of hole, as in elastic or rope fastenings. Outgrown clothing can be mounted to make extra buttoning boards.

Comments

Be certain there are generous openings to fit the buttons. Snug fittings may be needed on real garments but this practice board has success as its first priority!

40 CLOSE IT UP
Grippers and Hooks

AREA

Personal: Self-care

PURPOSE

To try a variety of garment fastenings such as gripper snaps and hooks and eyes.

Place in Development

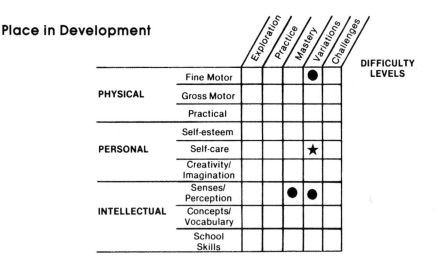

		Exploration	Practice	Mastery	Variations	Challenges	DIFFICULTY LEVELS
PHYSICAL	Fine Motor				●		
	Gross Motor						
	Practical						
PERSONAL	Self-esteem						
	Self-care				★		
	Creativity/ Imagination						
INTELLECTUAL	Senses/ Perception			●	●		
	Concepts/ Vocabulary						
	School Skills						

Other Areas: Physical: Fine Motor

Specific Value

Children love manageable and sensible new challenges. After struggling and succeeding with zippers, buckles, and buttons, these gripper snaps and hooks and eyes will provide a pleasant diversion into additional but similar activities. Mastery of gripper snaps and hooks and eyes are nonetheless valuable self-care skills needed for many types of clothing for children, their dolls, and other play accessories.

Child's Readiness

For children with limited skill abilities these materials will need to be held in reserve, while for skillful youngsters they can be attempted at the same time as buttons and buckles.

Applications

Older preschoolers will want to work very hard at these boards.
Even blind youngsters enjoy a challenge like this one.

Variations and Related Ideas

Assorted fabrics, snap and hook sizes, and garments can be used for these materials. The number of fasteners on the fabric can also be varied from two to eight or more. Children may enjoy challenging themselves on the time it takes to complete these materials. Teachers who have sewing skills may also wish to create story figures where coats are put on and removed following a story line.

Comments

Wear and tear is to be expected, and a sewing repair kit will likely be needed to maintain these materials.

41 LACING VEST

AREA

Personal: Self-care

PURPOSE

To understand and use laces for fastening.

Place in Development

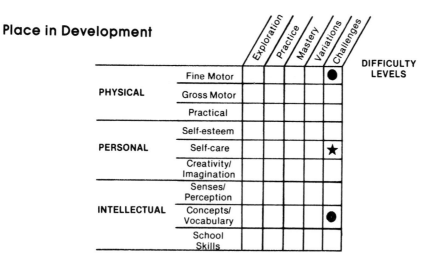

		Exploration	Practice	Mastery	Variations	Challenges	DIFFICULTY LEVELS
PHYSICAL	Fine Motor					●	
	Gross Motor						
	Practical						
PERSONAL	Self-esteem						
	Self-care					★	
	Creativity/ Imagination						
INTELLECTUAL	Senses/ Perception						
	Concepts/ Vocabulary					●	
	School Skills						

Other Areas: Physical; Intellectual

Specific Value

Lacing involves physical skills such as threading and tying but it also requires understanding the reversal of directions and criss-crossing operations used with these strings. It is a somewhat advanced, coordinated skill. The Lacing Vest can help the child to deal with these operations as they relate to clothing and/or a craft. Lots of practice is needed and a great many mistakes are to be expected, but this activity has valuable learning potential for both physical and perceptual skills.

Child's Readiness

The Lacing Vest is appropriate for children whose abilities in threading are established. Motivation is also important.

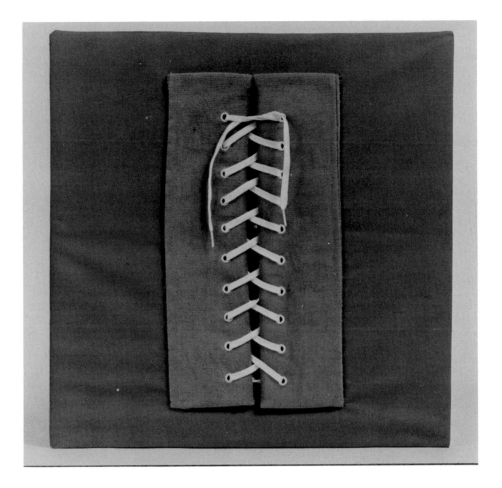

Applications

Older preschoolers able to persist with challenging tasks will enjoy this interesting and variable activity.

With appropriate physical skills any handicapped child can enjoy this activity, especially if he or she enjoys the challenge.

Variations and Related Ideas

The Lacing Vest can be changed somewhat by alternating the laces used and by adding real garments that close with laces. Cowboy or cowgirl types of clothing may still use laces and the children would enjoy identifying with these old fashioned heros.

Comments

Be certain that the metal or plastic lace ends are in good condition so that they move smoothly through the metal eyelets.

42 SHOE TYING

AREA

Personal: Self-care

PURPOSE

To learn to lace and tie shoes.

Place in Development

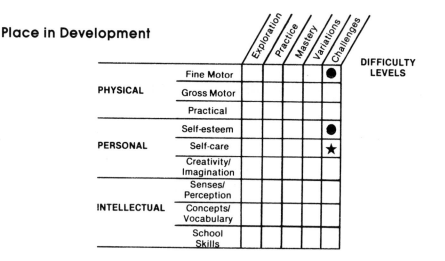

		Exploration	Practice	Mastery	Variations	Challenges	
PHYSICAL	Fine Motor					●	**DIFFICULTY LEVELS**
	Gross Motor						
	Practical						
PERSONAL	Self-esteem					●	
	Self-care					★	
	Creativity/ Imagination						
INTELLECTUAL	Senses/ Perception						
	Concepts/ Vocabulary						
	School Skills						

Other Areas: Physical; Self-esteem

Specific Value

Children love mastering the task of tying their own shoes. It brings independence and admiration from friends and adults; yet, when analyzed, the act of shoe tying consists of several difficult component tasks. The bow tie itself is the most taxing. It requires a good deal of coordination and concentration; the physical skills alone require repeated efforts at mastery. But once achieved, shoe tying is a basic and valued self-care activity.

Child's Readiness

Older preschool aged children are generally ready to achieve some success in shoe tying. Handicapped youngsters will need skills in eye-hand coordination. Motivation that lends persistence is another needed ingredient because this is a complex challenge.

Applications

Kindergarteners often are very motivated to achieve this "grown-up" task.
Older retarded children can practice this activity repeatedly in a relaxed framework.

Variations and Related Ideas

Real children's shoes, doll shoes, and grown-up shoes are enjoyable for practicing shoe tying. Commercial lacing shoes filled with small people figures can also be used. Children will need to think about right and left in this activity; some teachers like to indicate this in some way on the shoes themselves. The two-tone laces here will contribute to the child's understanding of the balance and sidedness involved in tying up one's shoes.

Comments

Some laces are too slippery and they don't remain snugly fastened. Long, soft, and well-maintained laces will ease the task.

43 FELT DRAWING

AREA

Personal: Creativity

PURPOSE

To explore the use of shapes to create designs.

Place in Development

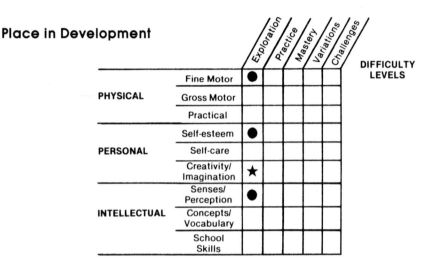

		Exploration	Practice	Mastery	Variations	Challenges	DIFFICULTY LEVELS
PHYSICAL	Fine Motor	●					
	Gross Motor						
	Practical						
PERSONAL	Self-esteem	●					
	Self-care						
	Creativity/Imagination	★					
INTELLECTUAL	Senses/Perception	●					
	Concepts/Vocabulary						
	School Skills						

Other Areas: Self-esteem; Sensory Experiences

Specific Value

Felt boards have, deservedly, been popular for years. The creative possibilities are wide yet the physical requirements are minimal. These characteristics make the Felt Drawing board especially valuable for the young or the handicapped child. The basic shapes and colors also build understandings around these concepts. The error-free quality makes the activity highly success-oriented and good for self-esteem. The variations are endless because the child's creative sense is the major focus.

Child's Readiness

Only minimal coordination skills are needed for these materials. The felt used here is quite nubby so that all shapes stick easily.

Applications

Any young child will enjoy this simple and colorful activity. The sticky felt quality is also very pleasant to work with.

The physically handicapped child will be able to express many creative ideas without having advanced physical skills.

Variations and Related Ideas

Several colors and shapes are needed for the Felt Drawing board. Beyond these, any sticky fabrics will enable the child to create delightful collages. Later, children can use figures of people and animals to design whole cities. The child who takes pride in his or her success will want to leave it untouched for a while, so several boards may be needed. Teachers can also discuss the results at length with the child. If an instant camera is available, the design can be kept and displayed!

Comments

Be sure that children are not expected to follow adult designs. A hodgepodge is more reflective of youngsters' thinking. Praise their interest and sense of design!

44 NAIL DRAWING

AREA

Personal: Creativity

PURPOSE

To try out and practice expressive designs with colored yarn.

Place in Development

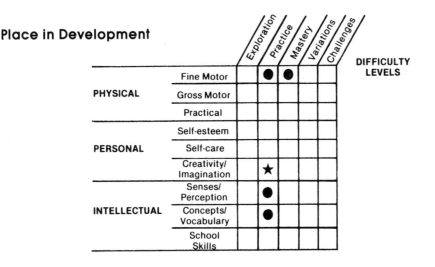

DIFFICULTY LEVELS

		Exploration	Practice	Mastery	Variations	Challenges
PHYSICAL	Fine Motor	●	●			
	Gross Motor					
	Practical					
PERSONAL	Self-esteem					
	Self-care					
	Creativity/ Imagination	★				
INTELLECTUAL	Senses/ Perception	●				
	Concepts/ Vocabulary	●				
	School Skills					

Other Areas: Physical: Fine Motor

Specific Value

Children love designs in which they can experiment. They also love a variety of art media from paper, to cloth, to wood. Colored yarn is a delight to work with—soft, pliant, and thick. Nails and wood have a very grown-up feeling for children. Together, children can use Nail Drawings to express ideas and images or create them as they go along. This is an open-ended, fun material, flexible enough to permit the child's imagination to seek out interesting designs of line and shape. No standards are set for judging the product. Satisfaction is built in. Physical skills also grow as the child weaves yarn in and about the nails. Because there is good feeling and success, you may be surprised by the diversity of design and the expressiveness of each child.

Child's Readiness

When the child seems able to succeed in winding yarn and takes pleasure in the visual display of color, line, and shape, this Nail Drawing board will be much enjoyed.

Applications

The preschool child will want to try out different materials and may even enjoy sharing the board with others in group collage.

The physically handicapped child is able to try many different designs and possibly use other materials. The rewards are immediate for this easy-to-use art media.

The deaf child may particularly appreciate the opportunity for nonverbal self-expression that others can easily relate to.

Variations and Related Ideas

Other materials can be used on the board, and the nails can be arranged in a variety of squares, circles, lines, or random patterns. Rubber bands, string, and cloth strips can be mixed with or used in place of yarn.

Comments

Once the child grasps the notion that this is an open, multidesign project, the creative urge will grow. Point out new possibilities if the child is stalled, such as other colors or methods for other configurations. Photographs of finished designs may even stimulate ideas for paintings or chalk designs that are similarly open-ended.

45 THREADING AROUND

AREA

Personal: Creativity

PURPOSE

To practice threading in a creative way.

Place in Development

		Exploration	Practice	Mastery	Variations	Challenges	DIFFICULTY LEVELS
PHYSICAL	Fine Motor	●	●				
	Gross Motor						
	Practical						
PERSONAL	Self-esteem						
	Self-care						
	Creativity/ Imagination		★				
INTELLECTUAL	Senses/ Perception			●			
	Concepts/ Vocabulary			●			
	School Skills						

Other Areas: Physical; Self-esteem

Specific Value

Many creative activities for children involve the use of yarn and holes. This activity will build the child's skills in negotiating yarn or string through a series of fixed and easily accessible holes. The corral-like quality encourages the child to persist until he or she completes the circle. Several colors and a few alternative design options add the creative touch. Criss-cross and cut-across designs are also possible.

Child's Readiness

Children who are physically able to get the leads through the first hole will enjoy continuing with the activity.

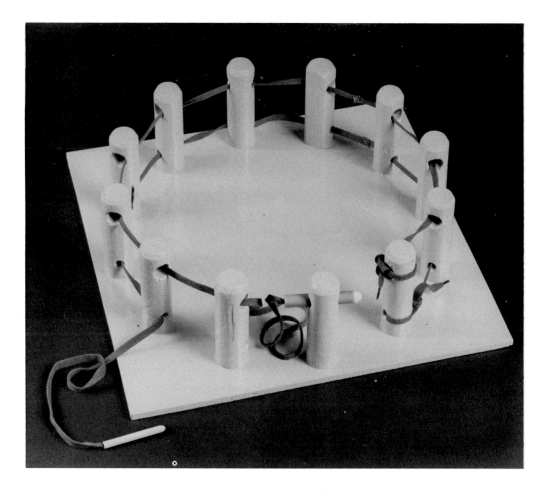

Applications

Children will appreciate the slight challenge in this material; it is unusual but manageable.

Physically handicapped children will appreciate the sturdy board and posts, especially if they are confined.

Variations and Related Ideas

Many varied yarns, shoelaces, strings, or ropes can be used for Threading Around. Adults may want to demonstrate different patterns in going around the circle. Some children will enjoy using the completed circle with rubber animal figures in a pretend zoo or corral. Several holes could be added. Children could also talk about the posts as figures in a circle playing ring-around games and could create some easy games.

Comments

The leads on the materials used for threading will need to be smooth and solid enough to be easily pushed into the holes.

46 WIRE WEAVING

AREA

Personal: Creativity

PURPOSE

To use a mesh surface to create woven designs.

Place in Development

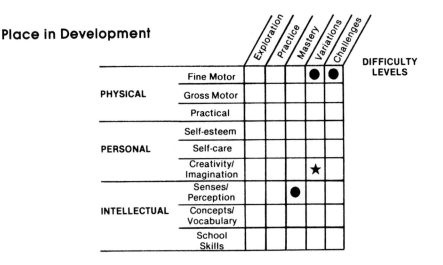

		Exploration	Practice	Mastery	Variations	Challenges	DIFFICULTY LEVELS
PHYSICAL	Fine Motor				●	●	
	Gross Motor						
	Practical						
PERSONAL	Self-esteem						
	Self-care						
	Creativity/ Imagination				★		
INTELLECTUAL	Senses/ Perception			●			
	Concepts/ Vocabulary						
	School Skills						

Other Areas: Physical; Sensory Experiences

Specific Value

Woven designs, rich in color and texture, are fascinating to children. They enjoy the tactile quality of the yarn and the sensory delight of a variety of colors. Wire Weaving is somewhat more difficult physically when there is a consistent movement in and out of the mesh, but children may try several creative possibilities using their own notions of weaving.

Child's Readiness

This is a somewhat advanced activity requiring some skill and understanding of threading. Less experienced children may enjoy exploring the materials if they do not become frustrated.

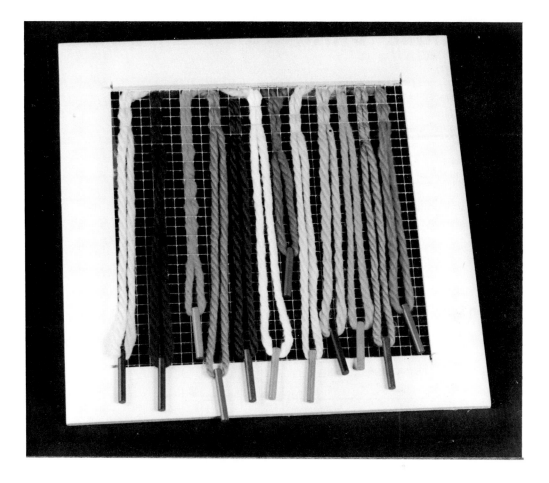

Applications

Even a group of children may enjoy working this board. They can watch each other in turn.

Older children who have the skills may wish to work extensively on this creative activity. It might even lead to permanent weavings.

Variations and Related Ideas

The Wire Weaving board can be used in varying sizes with differing strings, ropes or cloth strips. The resulting textures will be fascinating. If several children take turns working on a design, a good deal of friendly social interaction may occur. Any wonderful finished products could be kept by removing the mesh, but the creative process here is more important to the activity than the finished product.

Comments

Adults will need to model the weaving process to the children. The board also needs to be untangled when the yarns are too short to work with.

47 HOLE DRAWING

AREA

Personal: Creativity

PURPOSE

To use unusual materials in creative ways.

Place in Development

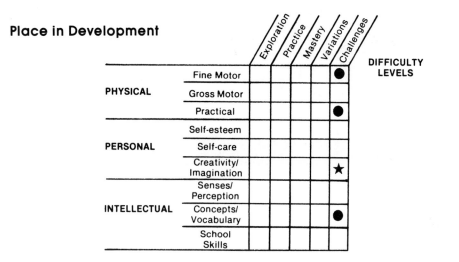

		Exploration	Practice	Mastery	Variations	Challenges	
PHYSICAL	Fine Motor					●	**DIFFICULTY LEVELS**
	Gross Motor						
	Practical					●	
PERSONAL	Self-esteem						
	Self-care						
	Creativity/Imagination					★	
INTELLECTUAL	Senses/Perception						
	Concepts/Vocabulary					●	
	School Skills						

Other Areas: Physical: Practical

Specific Value

This large peg-type board can be used to create a variety of designs with colored yarns or string. It is an enjoyable challenge for the creative child. It is also a pre-sewing activity in that simple basting stitches can be practiced.

Child's Readiness

The child who is able to use yarn effectively and understand how to make use of the alternating holes will enjoy this unusual board.

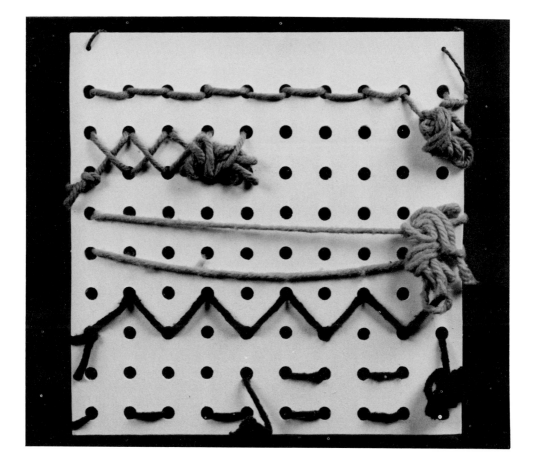

Applications

Older and more capable children will enjoy the uniqueness of this material. Toddlers will like poking through the holes.

Confined children can use this as a lap activity.

Variations and Related Ideas

The Hole Drawing board can be painted to create patterns resembling those for needlepoint. A plain background and different thicknesses of yarn do, however, permit the children to keep design options open. Their own ideas will determine many resulting designs.

Comments

The holes here need to accommodate the yarn with or without a threading needle.

III. INTELLECTUAL AREA OF DEVELOPMENT

In the child's early years the intellectual area of development is very much tied to concrete and personal experiences. Children spend a lot of time observing and interacting with a world of people and objects. Their encounters with materials contribute to a gradual, cyclical building up of ideas, words and perceptions. These experiences are building blocks in mental processes. It is seldom a passive kind of learning experience; it is an active one in which the child engages materials and uses several modes for taking in and intellectually organizing information. Activities 48 to 88 are primarily intellectual in focus.

Sensory experiences are one aspect of intellectual growth. Touching, seeing, and hearing activities serve to stimulate the mind and sort out perceptions of what is important or characteristic about this object or that series of events. Gradually the child remembers patterns and from these emerge ideas and understandings. Concept development is another aspect of intellectual growth. It includes vocabulary and information about how the world works. A wide variety of (eventually) academic activities can be introduced under this category. The third and most complex aspect of intellectual development is that of the "official" school skills such as reading, mathematics, and science. Beginning experiences with these subject areas are quite valuable for the young and handicapped, particularly when they are presented as interesting and satisfying materials.

Learning in the...

INTELLECTUAL AREA OF DEVELOPMENT

Aspects of Intellectual Growth

Levels of Difficulty	Sensory Experiences (Touching; Seeing; Hearing)	Concepts (Information; Vocabulary)	School Skills (Math; Reading; Science)
Exploration (getting acquainted with the materials)	48 / Fabric and Construction Circles 49 / Hubcap Sounds and Washboard Rhythms	60 / Color Lotto and Color Sort 61 / Big and Small Book 62 / Rings n' Things 63 / Little-Lot Book	76 / Amounts Lotto 77 / Counting Book 78 / Shapes Lotto and Shapes Board
Practice (experimenting and trying)	50 / Double Chimes 51 / Light and Dark Book 52 / Wallpaper Sorter	64 / Button Shop 65 / Round Book 66 / Basic Shapes Board 67 / Pairs Book	79 / Penny Board and Penny Book 80 / Number Writer
Study and mastery (succeeding or understanding)	53 / Touch Me Board 54 / Bells and Whistles/ Kitchen Sounds	68 / Graduated Lengths 69 / Bottle Tops 70 / Nuts and Bolts	81 / Magnet Board 82 / Magnifier 83 / Alphabet Objects
Variations (trying other ideas)	55 / Smell Jars 56 / Taste Jars	71 / Wide and Narrow Book 72 / Washer Drop and Squares Drop	84 / Signs Book 85 / Timers 86 / Bucket and Balance Scales
Challenges (advanced or complex skills)	57 / Mystery Bags 58 / Book of Surfaces 59 / Shaker Shop	73 / Clock 74 / Calendar 75 / Weather Board	87 / Grocery Store 88 / Bank Box

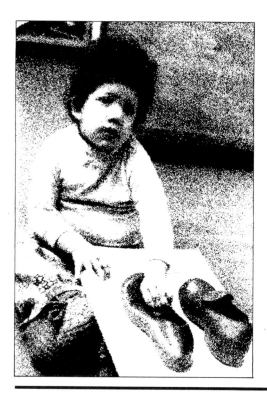

48 FABRIC AND CONSTRUCTION CIRCLES

AREA

Intellectual: Sensory

PURPOSE

To explore an assortment of varied round textures and colored designs by seeing and touching.

Place in Development

		Exploration	Practice	Mastery	Variations	Challenges
PHYSICAL	Fine Motor	●				
	Gross Motor	●				
	Practical					
PERSONAL	Self-esteem					
	Self-care					
	Creativity/ Imagination					
INTELLECTUAL	Senses/ Perception	★				
	Concepts/ Vocabulary	●				
	School Skills					

DIFFICULTY LEVELS

Other Areas: Physical; Gross Motor

Specific Value

The rich variety of textures and designs that children can touch and feel provide many opportunities for learning to discriminate sensory qualities, finding words to describe sensations, and dealing with notions of shape and color. The touch and feel quality here is wonderfully inviting—children and adults want to touch, want to talk about it. It's an invitation to learn in a very natural way. This is the kind of learning that stays with a child and spreads to other experiences with fabrics and textures. The child can also compare and point out details, thus forming building blocks of intelligence. Adults can help by asking questions and being available for comments; indeed, this mediation will greatly enhance the children's learning.

Child's Readiness

Any child can become happily engaged in this open-ended experience. Each will derive different ideas and concepts, depending on the particular child's interest and ability.

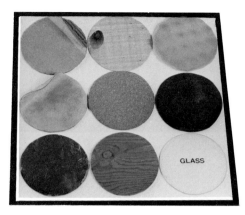

Applications

The youngest children will delight in touching, rubbing, fingering, and vocalizing about this array of fabric circles.

The blind children enjoy this just-for-touching experience. Adults can stand by to help the child think about the experience.

Retarded children can learn a series of concepts based on these real and immediate sensory experiences.

Variations and Related Ideas

Fabrics can be changed and moved about the board. Varying shapes might be used. These changes will stimulate children to reinvestigate the board every time they notice a difference. Games of "what's missing?" or "which is softest?" can be used to extend the child's concepts.

Comments

The adult's role includes helping the children to use labels and concepts as they are engaged in this exploration. You can add or withdraw challenges based upon the child's interest in your suggestions.

49 HUBCAP SOUNDS AND WASHBOARD RHYTHMS

AREA

Intellectual: Sensory Experiences

PURPOSE

To explore sounds and variations in sound patterns.

Place in Development

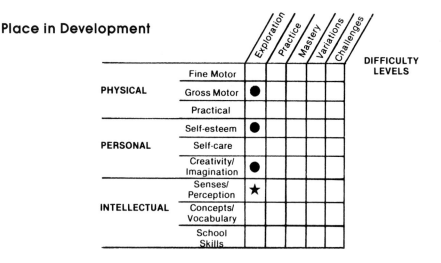

		Exploration	Practice	Mastery	Variations	Challenges	DIFFICULTY LEVELS
PHYSICAL	Fine Motor						
	Gross Motor	●					
	Practical						
PERSONAL	Self-esteem	●					
	Self-care						
	Creativity/ Imagination	●					
INTELLECTUAL	Senses/ Perception	★					
	Concepts/ Vocabulary						
	School Skills						

Other Areas: Physical; Self-esteem

Specific Value

When children are successful in making sounds they feel pleased. Soon they begin to alter the patterns in which they create these sounds. Such activities are stimulating to the senses and the mind. Often you can see the concentration and the interest in listening to and duplicating sounds. Physical skills are also involved in that children must coordinate hand and arm movements to strike or rub an object across a surface. The use of these real materials makes sound exploration very inviting!

Child's Readiness

These materials are appropriate for any child because few physical skills are required.

Applications

The youngest toddler appreciates this robust game. Older preschoolers will see it as a rhythm instrument.

Even severely handicapped and autistic children can use these materials successfully. They are quite appropriate for getting children to be active.

Variations and Related Ideas

Once the child happily explores sounds and rhythms with these materials, he or she may enjoy extending the activity to homemade drums, bells, or other types of banging and shaking noisemakers. Some purchased rhythm instruments would be a delightful part of sound and music experiences. Songs and games can be added using a piano, autoharp, or a record player. After the child seems saturated with free exploration, adults can ask them to make an effort to duplicate sound patterns modeled by others. This is an enjoyable memory task.

Comments

The joy of soundmaking sometimes taxes the ears! Perhaps a special noisy playtime can be reserved for this type of activity if your ears complain.

50 DOUBLE CHIMES

AREA

Intellectual: Sensory

PURPOSE

To practice creating and distinguishing musical sounds.

Place in Development

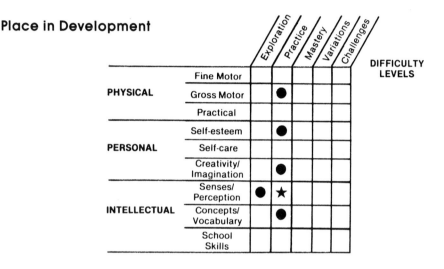

		Exploration	Practice	Mastery	Variations	Challenges	
PHYSICAL	Fine Motor						**DIFFICULTY LEVELS**
	Gross Motor	●					
	Practical						
PERSONAL	Self-esteem		●				
	Self-care						
	Creativity/ Imagination		●				
INTELLECTUAL	Senses/ Perception	●	★				
	Concepts/ Vocabulary		●				
	School Skills						

Other Areas: Creativity; Self-esteem

Specific Value

The lovely sounds created by bamboo and brass chimes are, in themselves, satisfying to produce. The child who listens to different sounds, who hears the timbre and the highs and lows, is also engaging in sensory perception and discrimination. In some ways, Double Chimes is a musical experience; but it also builds the child's intellectual understanding by stimulating the senses and keeping the mind active. What sounds are made by using a spoon or a wooden hammer? Why does a thick brass chime sound different from a thin one?

Child's Readiness

Double Chimes is an open activity, easy to use and capable of variations that reflect children's different activity and interest levels.

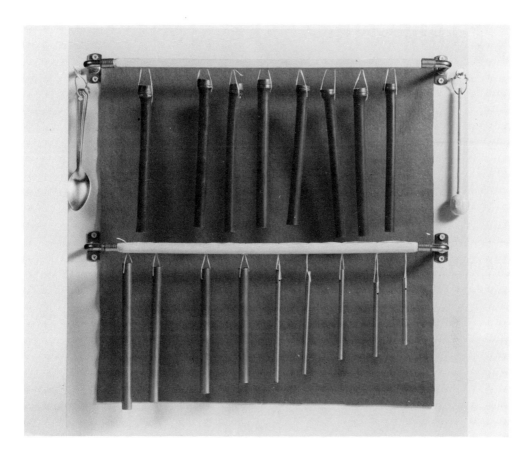

Applications

A child at any age can enjoy these chimes. They are simple to use but complex in effect.

Blind children might particularly appreciate these materials, as will cerebral palsied children whose coordination problems will not prevent some success.

Variations and Related Ideas

Many different materials can be mounted on this board as well, from rubber bands to violin strings. Strikers of varying materials might include plastic or a padded stick. The child can use the materials alone or the adult can demonstrate the musical and sound characteristics of each, comparing them to instruments used in an orchestra. The very musical child may even attempt to duplicate the tones made by the graduated brass chimes.

Comments

Once children become accustomed to listening carefully, they will appreciate the sound as well as the visual movement qualities or swinging of the chimes that may first attract them.

51 LIGHT AND DARK BOOK

AREA

Intellectual: Sensory

PURPOSE

To explore and practice perceptions of light and dark.

Place in Development

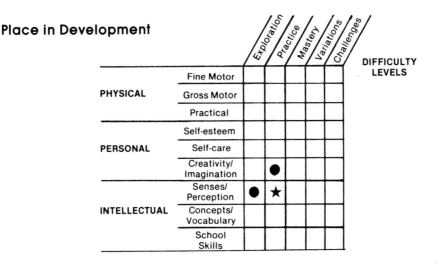

		Exploration	Practice	Mastery	Variations	Challenges	
PHYSICAL	Fine Motor						DIFFICULTY LEVELS
	Gross Motor						
	Practical						
PERSONAL	Self-esteem						
	Self-care						
	Creativity/ Imagination		●				
INTELLECTUAL	Senses/ Perception	●	★				
	Concepts/ Vocabulary						
	School Skills						

Other Areas: Concepts; School Skills

Specific Value

Colors are important in the life of the growing child. This includes perceiving them, telling them apart from one another, naming them, and simply enjoying them. Sometimes there is confusion when colors vary in hue. The study of colors is a delightful kind of learning, one made even more enjoyable by using an oversized book with removable "pages." The emphasis on light and dark will contribute to intellectual growth in that children learn to apply the concept to the variety of colors they encounter daily.

Child's Readiness

On one level, the child can explore these materials in a general way, while later they can use the corresponding descriptive words.

Applications

Most children will enjoy sorting through these pages.
Educable mentally retarded children may profit from repeated use of this book.

Variations and Related Ideas

The colors and papers used for these materials can be alternated. So, too, can the manner in which they are used—by individual children, in a group, or within a game format. Commercial color books and children's own smaller versions of this activity can complement what is used at school.

Comments

Adults may need to provide names for the colors and light-dark pages until the children are able to do this for themselves. Errors should be corrected before the child has a chance to learn a wrong color-name association.

52 WALLPAPER SORTER

AREA

Intellectual: Sensory

PURPOSE

To practice distinguishing and matching varied patterns.

Place in Development

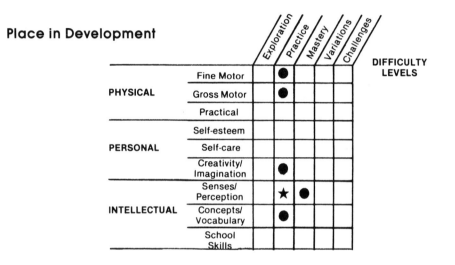

		Exploration	Practice	Mastery	Variations	Challenges	DIFFICULTY LEVELS
PHYSICAL	Fine Motor	●					
	Gross Motor	●					
	Practical						
PERSONAL	Self-esteem						
	Self-care						
	Creativity/ Imagination	●					
INTELLECTUAL	Senses/ Perception	★	●				
	Concepts/ Vocabulary	●					
	School Skills						

Other Areas: Creativity; Motor Development

Specific Value

When children are able to perceive and match patterns, they are demonstrating some basic thinking skills. Sorting activities help to build up the child's ability to notice form, shape, size, and other two-dimensional characteristics. In the Wallpaper Sorter the child's matching task is less taxing than it often is for similar but more complicated materials. Here, the child's confidence can be encouraged, as can his or her motor skills. Creativity is a factor because of the exposure to interesting patterns which the child may wish to try with paper and crayon. The visual display is also quite pleasing to the senses.

Child's Readiness

This activity is appropriate for children who are just beginning to understand the notion of finding a match or seeing the same design in a different place.

Applications

Young children will delight in finding the twins for each design or even sorting them along a table top.

Deaf and retarded children can learn a great deal about shapes and colors while using these materials.

Variations and Related Ideas

Wallpaper designs are almost infinite in their variety. The cards for the Wallpaper Sorter could be changed regularly. Textured designs, with flocking, would add a wonderful "feel" to the sorting task. The cards themselves could also be varied in size and shape. Just as children will use their imagination in dealing with the designs they encounter, so also can the adults use imagination in locating new and dramatic patterns!

Comments

Note the loops attached to the cards; these make the task of hanging them up a slightly challenging but satisfying one.

53 TOUCH ME BOARD

AREA

Intellectual: Sensory

PURPOSE

To explore and master concepts of texture in natural objects.

Place in Development

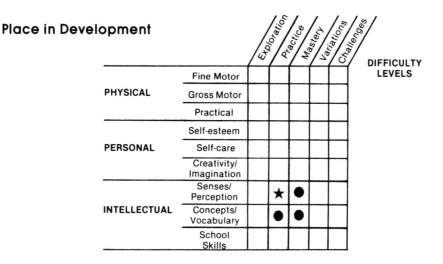

		Exploration	Practice	Mastery	Variations	Challenges	
							DIFFICULTY LEVELS
PHYSICAL	Fine Motor						
	Gross Motor						
	Practical						
PERSONAL	Self-esteem						
	Self-care						
	Creativity/ Imagination						
INTELLECTUAL	Senses/ Perception	★	●				
	Concepts/ Vocabulary	●	●				
	School Skills						

Other Areas: Information; Vocabulary

Specific Value

Nature is generous, indeed, in providing a wide array of hands-on materials from which children can learn. To build up the sensory and verbal experiences that contribute to intelligence, collections of objects found in the environment can be used extensively by children. Touching and feeling rough and smooth textures in similar shells, wood, rocks, weeds, and gourds is emphasized here. While the children master this concept, they are exploring ideas about the origins, uses, and other properties of these delightful materials. This activity integrates learning in many different preacademic areas.

Child's Readiness

Children can explore the Touch Me Board at any level; they can gain vocabulary and conceptual information as well when they are able to discuss the items.

Applications

All young children enjoy touching and feeling these materials. "Nature study" comes very natural to them.

Youngsters with language delays can use consistent words and phrases with these materials.

Blind children will have a delightful time experiencing these three-dimensional objects with other senses.

Variations and Related Ideas

Because nature has provided built-in appeal in its materials for children, virtually any such objects can be used for the Touch Me Board. Leaves, nuts, bark, and even dried flowers all come in a variety of colors, shapes and surfaces. The placement of smooth and rough items next to one another will help the children to more completely understand this sensory and intellectual concept. Magnifying glasses and color paddles will add an extra dimension to their study of these materials. Why not add several nature walks to your agenda and add to your collection?

Comments

Once collections of objects are started, it is hard to break the habit! Shoe box assortments from family outings can mushroom into file drawers full of explorable odds and ends!

54 BELLS AND WHISTLES/ KITCHEN SOUNDS

AREA

Intellectual: Sensory

PURPOSE

To succeed in creating and listening to a variety of common sounds.

Place in Development

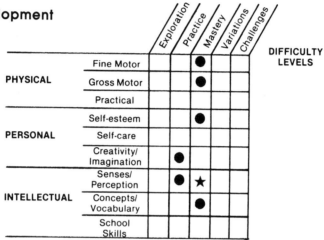

		Exploration	Practice	Mastery	Variations	Challenges	
PHYSICAL	Fine Motor		●				DIFFICULTY LEVELS
	Gross Motor		●				
	Practical						
PERSONAL	Self-esteem		●				
	Self-care						
	Creativity/ Imagination	●					
INTELLECTUAL	Senses/ Perception	●	★				
	Concepts/ Vocabulary		●				
	School Skills						

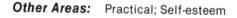

Other Areas: Practical; Self-esteem

Specific Value

Everyday sounds occurring within our immediate environment are frequent and interesting enough to stimulate the senses and encourage beginning thinking processes. Children enjoy exploring noisy objects; they can also learn to discriminate various types of sounds and study how they are created. These hands-on activities are successful for them, building the child's practical skills and feelings of competence and confidence—all of this with relatively simple and easily available materials! Vocabulary can be enhanced by encouraging the children to label the materials; physical skills are extended at the same time.

Child's Readiness

These materials are appropriate at the earliest levels of sensorimotor skills. If used for discrimination or labeling activities, the level is slightly higher but nonetheless easily managed.

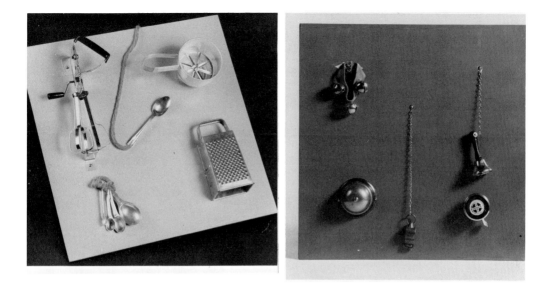

Applications

Even young toddlers will delight in creating these sounds, indeed they are a speciality for them!

Blind children will particularly enjoy practicing with these materials.

Cerebral palsied youngsters can enjoy the activity despite some of their difficulties in coordination.

Variations and Related Ideas

In addition to the bells and whistles displayed here, a variety of horns, rattles and other types of bells can be used. Kitchen utensils can be varied as well (nutcracker, lemon squeezer, etc.). One very popular game children enjoy is to hide their eyes, listen, and guess the sound. They can attempt to describe the sound in detail using words, and in turn build up the vocabulary of everyone in the group. They can create a simple book with pictures or they can tape-record the sounds and use them to develop a silly story.

Comments

Watch for fingers that may get in the way here, especially when wheels are turning!

55 SMELL JARS

AREA

Intellectual: Sensory

PURPOSE

To use the sense of smell to discriminate substances and label them.

Place in Development

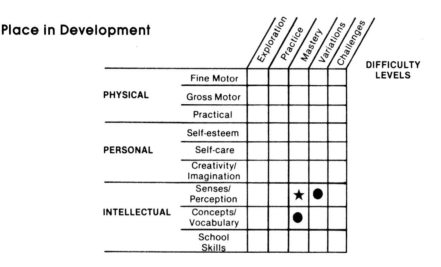

		Exploration	Practice	Mastery	Variations	Challenges	
PHYSICAL	Fine Motor						DIFFICULTY LEVELS
	Gross Motor						
	Practical						
PERSONAL	Self-esteem						
	Self-care						
	Creativity/ Imagination						
INTELLECTUAL	Senses/ Perception			★	●		
	Concepts/ Vocabulary			●			
	School Skills						

Other Areas: Vocabulary; School Skills

Specific Value

Some senses are seldom used in a conscious way as a means of attending to and analyzing information. The sense of smell can provide some entertaining and enlightening experiences. Not only can children gain in understanding the different qualities of substances but they can also learn to use their senses in ways that build their perceptions and their vocabulary. These fascinating Smell Jars form the basis for interesting experiences with prereading skills. Children can learn to attend to the written information on jars and labels. Matching activities can be developed around these words and substances to exercise the skills further.

Child's Readiness

Children who are able to handle substances cautiously without mouthing or spilling them will be able to explore these materials safely.

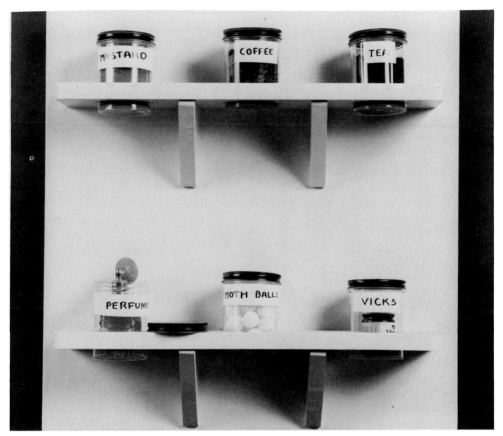

Applications

Older preschool children will enjoy this variation in using the senses; indeed, they
will also want to try out their perceptions at home.
Children with language problems will be very motivated to express their impressions.
Blind and physically handicapped youngsters can very much appreciate this activity.
It is easy to use and delightful in effect.

Variations and Related Ideas

Many different substances can be used for Smell Jars. Vanilla and other extracts are
wonderful, and only a few drops in a jar are necessary. Other spices such as basil,
dill, cinnamon, and cloves are equally interesting. The language component of this
activity cannot be overemphasized. Children will want to talk about all the things that
smells bring to mind. You might even keep a diary of some of their delightful expressions!

Comments

There is a safety consideration to these materials that needs planning and supervision. Children need to learn to smell the items cautiously and avoid mouthing or spilling them. Only safe substances should be used for the activity.

56 TASTE JARS

AREA

Intellectual: Sensory

PURPOSE

To use the sense of taste to study the qualities of substances.

Place in Development

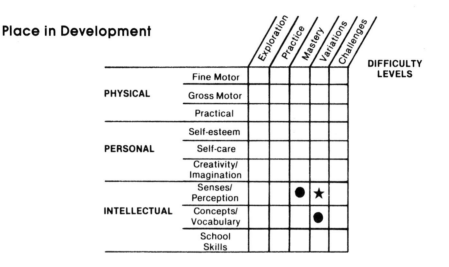

		Exploration	Practice	Mastery	Variations	Challenges	DIFFICULTY LEVELS
PHYSICAL	Fine Motor						
	Gross Motor						
	Practical						
PERSONAL	Self-esteem						
	Self-care						
	Creativity/ Imagination						
INTELLECTUAL	Senses/ Perception			●	★		
	Concepts/ Vocabulary				●		
	School Skills						

Other Areas: Vocabulary; Self-esteem

Specific Value

From infancy onward, children use their mouths and sense of taste to explore and discriminate everything from rattles to foods. For a child, tastes are very important. Why not use this natural affinity to help the child learn and develop in the sensory and intellectual areas? Activities in which distinct tastes are compared and analyzed will build these skills while providing an enjoyable experience for the youngster. Words should be used to label everything; picture books and play grocery stores can extend the learning to much higher levels.

Child's Readiness

Because of the child's ingestion of the materials in the taste jars, this activity should be reserved for later stages of personal self-control and ability to manage these tastes in sample form without consuming too much or choking.

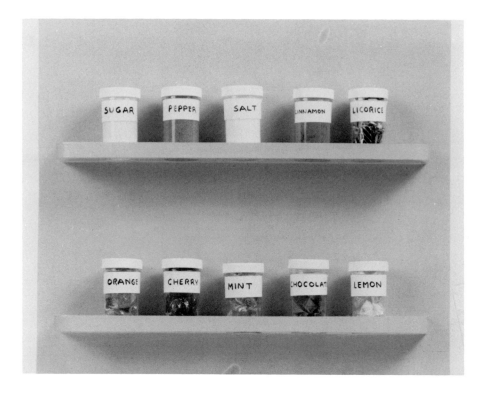

Applications

Older preschoolers will appreciate the fun of this taste testing. They can also understand some safety and nutrition concepts.

Blind and deaf children may particularly enjoy activities using the sense of taste.

Variations and Related Ideas

Once children seem comfortable with the notion of sampling tastes and talking
about them in detail, then a variety of tasting experiences can be planned during their
regular snack times. A tasting fair can be supported by parents who will be pleased
to supply small amounts of varied fruits, vegetables, cheeses, spreads, pickles,
breads, etc. The learning can and should be expanded to reading and math activities
using beginning skills to count and read, and information about obtaining and using
these items. A restaurant game will add lots of extra fun.

Comments

Children who can see these materials will want them—supplies of the sweeter
samples will quickly diminish! A special time for the activity may need to be planned,
such as after lunch.

57 MYSTERY BAGS

AREA

Intellectual: Sensory

PURPOSE

To use the sense of touch to identify hidden objects.

Place in Development

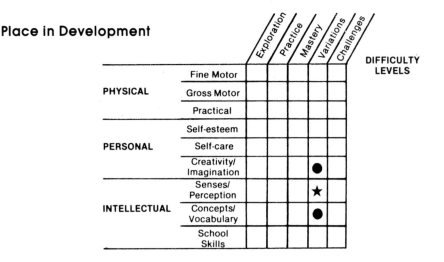

		Exploration	Practice	Mastery	Variations	Challenges	
							DIFFICULTY LEVELS
PHYSICAL	Fine Motor						
	Gross Motor						
	Practical						
PERSONAL	Self-esteem						
	Self-care						
	Creativity/ Imagination				●		
INTELLECTUAL	Senses/ Perception				★		
	Concepts/ Vocabulary				●		
	School Skills						

Other Areas: Vocabulary; Creativity

Specific Value

Guessing games are always popular with children, but this one has a unique twist. The Mystery Bags are filled with sets of objects that children can talk about, categorize, and sort once they have been identified. Children's intellect and memory are further stimulated by the requirement that they represent the objects in their mind, that they visualize them in order to identify them. Vocabulary is built up by using words while examining the materials. The child's creative mind is stimulated through imaginative games associated with guessing what an object is or what you do with it. To top it all off, emptying and filling bags is fun.

Child's Readiness

Mystery Bags can be used when children seem able to stop and think about something before they actually acquire it, that is, when mystery is not frustrating but exciting.

Applications

Most children enjoy the peekaboo nature of these materials and the mystery process as well.

Physically handicapped children will be motivated to persist in opening the bags and handling the objects or they can use them closed up.

Variations and Related Ideas

Any set of small, shaped objects that can be deciphered by touch are appropriate for the Mystery Bags. The challenge here is to entice the child to think about things they cannot see and to enjoy the sense of discovery and success when these sensory perceptions are correct. At a more difficult level, plastic animals, rubber people, and small cars and trucks can be identified by blind investigation with the fingers. Games might include "what is it?"; "what does it do?"; "how could you play with it?"; and other creative verbal activities in a small group.

Comments

Children will learn to take good care of the Mystery Bags if they are helped to keep them organized with the appropriate bags and hooks.

58 BOOK OF SURFACES

AREA

Intellectual: Sensory

PURPOSE

To use the senses of touch and sight to discriminate and compare surfaces.

Place in Development

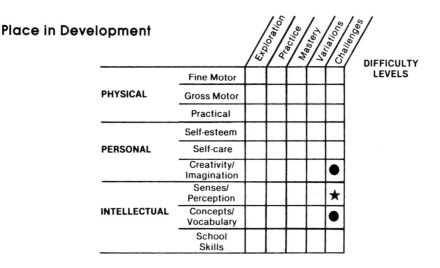

		Exploration	Practice	Mastery	Variations	Challenges	DIFFICULTY LEVELS
PHYSICAL	Fine Motor						
	Gross Motor						
	Practical						
PERSONAL	Self-esteem						
	Self-care						
	Creativity/ Imagination					●	
INTELLECTUAL	Senses/ Perception					★	
	Concepts/ Vocabulary					●	
	School Skills						

Other Areas: Vocabulary; Concepts

Specific Value

Surfaces are all around us but seldom do we stop to examine them closely. In this activity children are able to use two sensory modalities to examine substances they encounter on a regular basis. To concentrate on them in this context may enable children to be more alert to their environment on other occasions. These materials are also sources of vocabulary growth and of concept development concerning the uses of the items represented, their actual use in construction, etc.

Child's Readiness

Children at several levels can explore these surfaces, but more experienced children will be able to extend their understanding beyond the materials at hand.

Applications

Older preschool children will relate to the real-world uses of these materials; they can understand their functions in other settings.

Language-delayed children can use this activity to build their expressive vocabulary.

Variations and Related Ideas

Because these materials are extracted from the real world they can also serve as a link back to it. Cardboard, cork, wood, styrofoam, and foil can be gathered and used for collage pictures with paper or three-dimensional constructions requiring glue or nails. The project can be extended to include a trip to a building under repair or construction or to a building supplies dealer. Add a story about the experience and it's a natural early reading book.

Comments

Words are important here and children should learn to use the appropriate labels.

59 SHAKER SHOP

AREA

Intellectual: Sensory

PURPOSE

To use several senses to think about the qualities of substances.

Place in Development

		Exploration	Practice	Mastery	Variations	Challenges	DIFFICULTY LEVELS
PHYSICAL	Fine Motor						
	Gross Motor						
	Practical						
PERSONAL	Self-esteem					●	
	Self-care						
	Creativity/ Imagination						
INTELLECTUAL	Senses/ Perception					★	
	Concepts/ Vocabulary					●	
	School Skills						

Other Areas: Motor; Vocabulary

Specific Value

From the time a child first shakes a rattle, there is a great deal of interest in how things look, sound and act when they are vigorously explored. The materials in the Shaker Shop will arouse children's curiosity and satisfy their desire to hear what they see. The self-contained nature of the activity only adds to the intrigue about what will result. Words and conversation help the children express their impressions while the box-like container serves to store and attract children at the same time. Indeed the "shop" notion is fun for everyone.

Child's Readiness

Children need minimal physical skills for the Shaker Shop but they also should be tolerant of their inability to uncover the jars!

Applications

Young children will love the action-oriented nature—the invitation of this activity to be involved beyond looking.

Any handicapped child, particularly the deaf youngster, will enjoy this delightful feast for the eyes.

Variations and Related Ideas

Man and nature have provided a good many resources for these materials. Pick something widely appealing to the young to vary these jars, the noisier the better. Games can be used for a small group, but individual exploration with labels supplied by adults is highly valuable. Later, the children might try to remember what was there and how it acted when it shook! A collection of samples could be retained with written words as a prereading activity.

Comments

Unbreakable jars are important for vigorous shaking!

60 COLOR LOTTO AND COLOR SORT

AREA

Intellectual: Concepts

PURPOSE

To match and label colors and explore the concept of color.

Place in Development

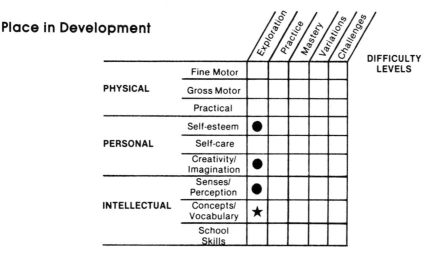

DIFFICULTY LEVELS

		Exploration	Practice	Mastery	Variations	Challenges
PHYSICAL	Fine Motor					
	Gross Motor					
	Practical					
PERSONAL	Self-esteem	●				
	Self-care					
	Creativity/ Imagination	●				
INTELLECTUAL	Senses/ Perception	●				
	Concepts/ Vocabulary	★				
	School Skills					

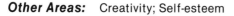

Other Areas: Creativity; Self-esteem

Specific Value

Children enjoy activities that enable them to find a match between similar colors or shapes. The Color Lotto and Color Sort are large and easy to use. They will help the child to understand how to sort and match objects by their qualities. It is a thinking skill in that the child has to use perception and memory. It also builds up conceptual understanding in its requirement for dealing with color as a category by which to classify objects. Color is also important to the creative process and children's delight in using it for many activities will be apparent throughout the school years. Color sorting is, in addition, a success-oriented activity designed to build esteem and confidence while learning about concepts.

Child's Readiness

Children able to distinguish colors from one another can manage these materials with little supervision beyond an initial demonstration of how to match the circles and squares.

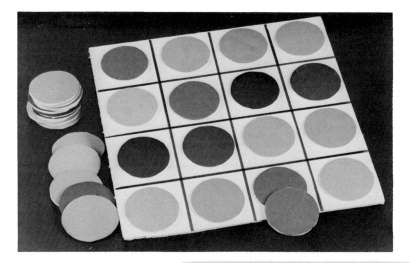

Applications

Young preschoolers will enjoy the fun of sorting colors, especially the good feeling that comes from seeing the matched sets.

Retarded children can gain a thorough understanding of color with these materials.

Variations and Related Ideas

The Color Lotto and Color Sort can be varied in their use of specific sets of colors. The school calendar is one organizer of color experiences. It may begin with primary colors, then fall colors, holiday reds and greens, pastel spring colors, etc. A wide range of graduated hues may also be used. The neighborhood paint shop is an excellent source of sample color cards containing virtually endless arrays of similar colors. Many children's games and special activities carry color themes, i.e., weekly colors, songs about colors in clothes, "I spy a color" games, paint and colored water mixing, etc.

Comments

Colors on paper tend to fade with exposure to light. Be sure your squares and lotto board and individual circles contain the same colors!

61 BIG AND SMALL BOOK

AREA

Intellectual: Concepts

PURPOSE

To explore size concepts using common objects.

Place in Development

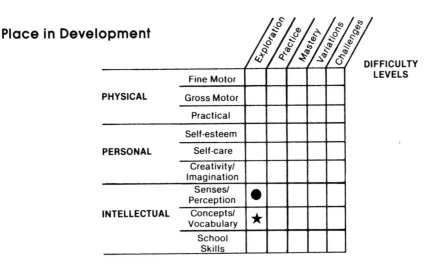

		Exploration	Practice	Mastery	Variations	Challenges	DIFFICULTY LEVELS
PHYSICAL	Fine Motor						
	Gross Motor						
	Practical						
PERSONAL	Self-esteem						
	Self-care						
	Creativity/ Imagination						
INTELLECTUAL	Senses/ Perception	●					
	Concepts/ Vocabulary	★					
	School Skills						

Other Areas: Vocabulary; Sensory Perception

Specific Value

One of children's most commonly used conceptual distinctions is that of size—of how big or small something is. It is a comparative characteristic because of the relative use of these terms and the need for standards to judge the size of something. Size can also be applied to almost anything regardless of color or shape, and vocabulary is easily attached. The Big and Small Book is immediately attractive to children because it uses common, as well as popular, items to study this concept. The child is able to use his or her senses to explore and then describe size, texture, shape, and object uses with words.

Child's Readiness

This material is appropriate as an early experience in dealing with simple concepts.

Applications

Young preschoolers love the concept of big as applied here.
Retarded and blind children will appreciate the tactile reinforcement of this concept.

Variations and Related Ideas

Teachers and parents can select from a wide range of popular objects to use for the Big and Small Book. The search for duplicates with size differences is almost a treat for adults and children, especially if they join together for a scavenger hunt to collect them. The concept can be applied to the child's overall surroundings—chairs, plates, glasses, windows, etc. "Name-it" games can be used as well to encourage vocabulary development while applying size descriptors.

Comments

Outstanding size differences are the most entertaining for children!

62 RINGS N' THINGS

AREA

Intellectual: Concepts

PURPOSE

To explore, sort, and arrange materials by size and shape.

Place in Development

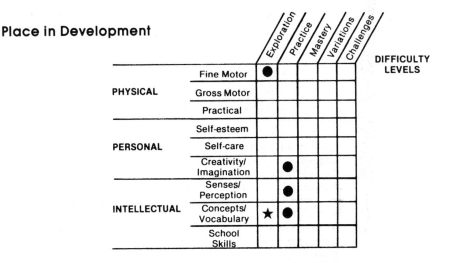

DIFFICULTY LEVELS

		Exploration	Practice	Mastery	Variations	Challenges
PHYSICAL	Fine Motor	●				
	Gross Motor					
	Practical					
PERSONAL	Self-esteem					
	Self-care					
	Creativity/ Imagination		●			
INTELLECTUAL	Senses/ Perception		●			
	Concepts/ Vocabulary	★	●			
	School Skills					

Other Areas: Physical; Creativity

Specific Value

The expression "beautiful junk" might be very appropriate for this appealing array of odd circular materials for children to sort and study. The intellectual processes used to perceive and arrange the rings are important, but it's always wonderful when a learning activity has a charm and appeal in and of itself. The structure in this task is simple and straightforward, with some accompanying physical skills involved. It is also somewhat creative in the design that can be produced over the entire board. Each child can make his or her own unique display—one that resembles a sculpture! Colors, shapes, materials, textures, and uniqueness in design can all be studied and discussed.

Child's Readiness

Once the child has passed the stage of mouthing small objects, these materials will provide their own "sort-me" messages. The appeal and the child's response to it will come naturally.

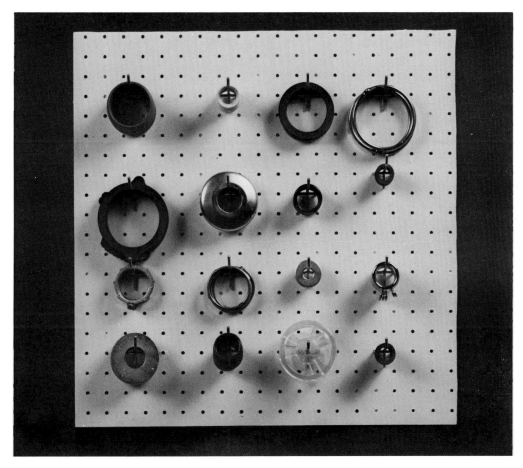

Applications

Preschoolers will love the "stuff" in this activity; they will want to add more of their own.

The application of shape concepts to real objects will reinforce this concept for retarded blind children.

Variations and Related Ideas

Anything goes in locating suitable circular objects for Rings n' Things. Start with a hardware store and don't overlook your neighbor's workbench. While this activity can be used by one or two children on their own, a small group game might include "What's missing" or "Find the smallest, hardest, etc." You might even wish to photograph the board in different arrays to demonstrate the creative potential in the task.

Comments

Be sure to use the word *circle*. Also, resist the temptation to provide a model for placing objects on a particular hook—let the child create. Watch for disappearing rings; try to keep them organized in sets.

63 LITTLE - LOT BOX

AREA

Intellectual: Concepts

PURPOSE

To explore concepts of amount.

Place in Development

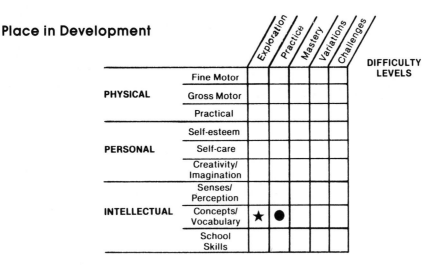

		Exploration	Practice	Mastery	Variations	Challenges	
PHYSICAL	Fine Motor						DIFFICULTY LEVELS
	Gross Motor						
	Practical						
PERSONAL	Self-esteem						
	Self-care						
	Creativity/ Imagination						
INTELLECTUAL	Senses/ Perception						
	Concepts/ Vocabulary	★	●				
	School Skills						

Other Areas: Vocabulary

Specific Value

The learning of mathematical concepts begins with notions such as a little bit and a lot of something, or few and many. From this beginning children better understand what counting means and how written numerals represent amounts. Tasks involving matching amounts are common in the early school years, but the Little-Lot Book provides a more primary approach to this concept. The materials here repeat and reinforce with a variety of applications from the real world. The use of these items also builds the child's vocabulary.

Child's Readiness

This activity is easy to use, requiring minimal physical skills and only beginning understandings of simple concepts.

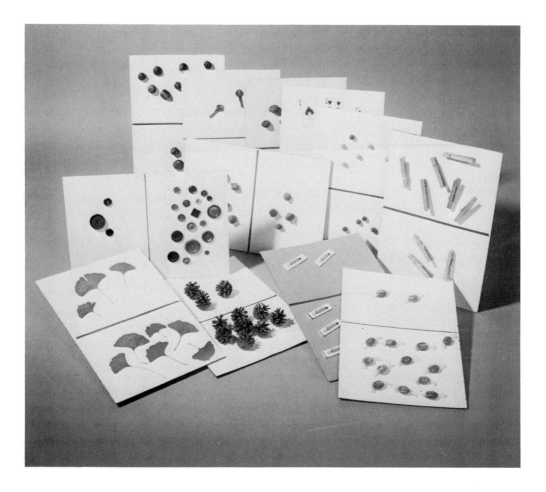

Applications

Any young child will enjoy touching and talking about these amounts.
The easy mastery here makes it very appropriate for the child with very limited abilities.

Variations and Related Ideas

Certainly adults can vary the particular items used for the Little-Lot Book. The "pages" of this book can be displayed together with those from other books. The children could then describe the concepts. Amounts can also be studied in relation to food servings, toy sets, and other aspects of the child's daily experience.

Comments

Items will need to be very firmly attached to withstand curious fingers. Only safe objects should be used.

64 BUTTON SHOP

AREA

Intellectual: Concepts

PURPOSE

To practice sorting objects by color.

Place in Development

		Exploration	Practice	Mastery	Variations	Challenges	DIFFICULTY LEVELS
PHYSICAL	Fine Motor	●					
	Gross Motor						
	Practical						
PERSONAL	Self-esteem	●					
	Self-care						
	Creativity/ Imagination						
INTELLECTUAL	Senses/ Perception	●					
	Concepts/ Vocabulary	★	●				
	School Skills						

Other Areas: Sensory Discrimination; Self-esteem

Specific Value

Object collections are always enjoyed by young children. The Button Shop is a delightful way to use these as a means of practicing how to find like objects and sort them into containers. The child is able to act on his or her discrimination in a concrete and pleasant way. The task is even more enjoyable because of the dramatic play involved in pretending to go to a Button Shop. Such play builds children's self-esteem through its childlike and open-ended nature. There is also a sense of satisfaction in placing buttons into these special cans with matching lids. To the child, this putting-it-away activity approximates the adult world and it feels good to do that.

Child's Readiness

Children who are able to relate to both colors and the use of separate containers will enjoy practicing this straightforward task. Minimal physical skills are required.

Applications

Preschoolers will love emptying and filling these containers, especially toddlers. Children with problems in coordination will delight in this success-oriented task. It is easy and fun.

Variations and Related Ideas

The Button Shop principle can be applied to other sets of objects such as small animals, pictures of fruits or vegetables, etc. Counting activities can be added once the child has had the opportunity to enjoy the sorting task. Eventually, color words could be used in place of the identifying colors on the cans, making reading a part of the challenge. The notion of shopping can also be extended to finding other objects to place in the can with a corresponding color. For younger children buttons should be large.

Comments

The noisy cans are especially satisfying to children as they drop in the matched button—this makes tin cans preferable to plastic. Be sure the lids are smooth and safe.

65 ROUND BOOK

AREA

Intellectual: Concepts

PURPOSE

To practice identifying round shapes in common objects.

Place in Development

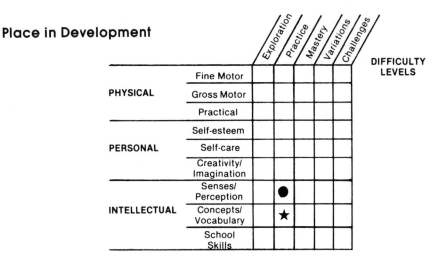

		Exploration	Practice	Mastery	Variations	Challenges
PHYSICAL	Fine Motor					
	Gross Motor					
	Practical					
PERSONAL	Self-esteem					
	Self-care					
	Creativity/ Imagination					
INTELLECTUAL	Senses/ Perception	●				
	Concepts/ Vocabulary	★				
	School Skills					

DIFFICULTY LEVELS

Other Areas: Vocabulary; Sensory Discrimination

Specific Value

The concept of shape is one that is basic to the child's preparation for reading and writing. The circle is a shape found everywhere in daily experiences. Children who are beginning to decipher these notions will take great pride in feeling the roundness of the objects on these "pages." The concept is reinforced through the senses and applied to common objects, yet the child's task is an appealing one because the materials are right at hand and comfortable to use. Vocabulary development is also enhanced because the situation invites the labeling of these items.

Child's Readiness

These materials are very appropriate at the beginning stages of shape recognition and language development; but there is some challenge in perceiving the consistent roundness in very different objects.

Applications

Many young children will enjoy discovering the round qualities in these materials. Children with physical handicaps can explore these objects easily; the "pages" are large and sturdy.

Variations and Related Ideas

The concept of shape can be explored by selecting many different ones, such as squares, rectangles, ovals, stars, diamonds, etc. In this way, the Round Book is only one of a possible series, each helping children to perceive shapes in the world around them. Children can extend their activity to collecting additional circular objects from their homes. A classroom collection box can be used on a weekly basis for such gathered items. A hide-and-seek game can also become a shape lesson with these materials. Eventually, children can write a story about circle families or adventures with shapes!

Comments

Family members enjoy helping children with these "home work" activities. It's a delightful way of getting involved in a learning adventure.

66 BASIC SHAPES BOARD

AREA

Intellectual: Concepts

PURPOSE

To practice matching basic shapes.

Place in Development

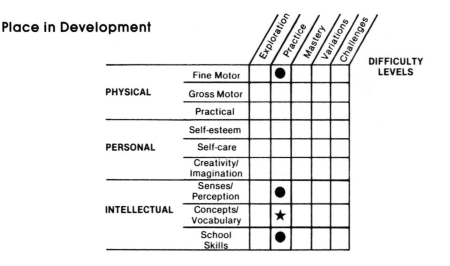

		Exploration	Practice	Mastery	Variations	Challenges
PHYSICAL	Fine Motor	●				
	Gross Motor					
	Practical					
PERSONAL	Self-esteem					
	Self-care					
	Creativity/Imagination					
INTELLECTUAL	Senses/Perception	●				
	Concepts/Vocabulary	★				
	School Skills	●				

DIFFICULTY LEVELS

Other Areas: School Skills; Physical Growth

Specific Value

Children's first exposure to the basic shapes may consist of simple puzzles, commercial books in which shapes are presented and named, or art experiences using colorful shapes. With the Basic Shapes Board, the child's task is to match a small number of different shapes to one another. In this way, children become familiar and comfortable with them in an easily mastered activity. They are also asked to hang up the cards holding these shapes, using a small hole and a simple hook. The physical component serves as a reinforcement for the child's correct identification. The labels for each shape should be practiced because these names are part of the child's learning sequence and will be used repeatedly in schoolwork.

Child's Readiness

In terms of the physical task, this activity is easier than other types of shape sorters; but its very openness means children should have some notions about shapes in order to benefit from their experience.

Applications

This thinking-doing task is a pleasant one for the young child, even at the early toddler stages.

The relaxed pace of this activity will make it comfortable for any handicapped child.

Variations and Related Ideas

The cards used for the Basic Shapes Board can be varied in complexity once children are able to sort by shape. Configurations of shapes can be created in duplicate for sorting. Children's own shape collages borrowed from cutting and pasting activities can be used in this way. Textured shapes are another possibility that also enhances use of the senses.

Comments

Unlike a puzzle, these materials are not self-correcting, so that children can match dissimilar shapes. Adult supervision will prevent children from learning incorrect labels.

67 PAIRS BOOK

AREA

Intellectual: Concepts

PURPOSE

To explore and practice the concept of sets of matched pairs.

Place in Development

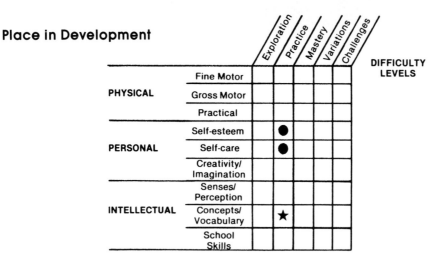

		Exploration	Practice	Mastery	Variations	Challenges
PHYSICAL	Fine Motor					
	Gross Motor					
	Practical					
PERSONAL	Self-esteem	●				
	Self-care	●				
	Creativity/Imagination					
INTELLECTUAL	Senses/Perception					
	Concepts/Vocabulary	★				
	School Skills					

DIFFICULTY LEVELS

Other Areas: Self-care; Self-esteem

Specific Value

The concept of belonging, of sets of items that go together, is in some ways a pre-mathematics understanding but also a practical one. Children enjoy the feeling of successfully caring for their own things and this ability begins with keeping track of pairs of mittens, shoes, etc. Many things come in 2's—especially body parts—so that this real-world understanding is a useful one. In early mathematical operations, many children will need to deal with sets of like items that are added or subtracted. The notion of pairs is a precursor to other intellectual tasks.

Child's Readiness

The Pairs Book requires few physical skills and presents a single, clear concept. This makes it appropriate at early levels.

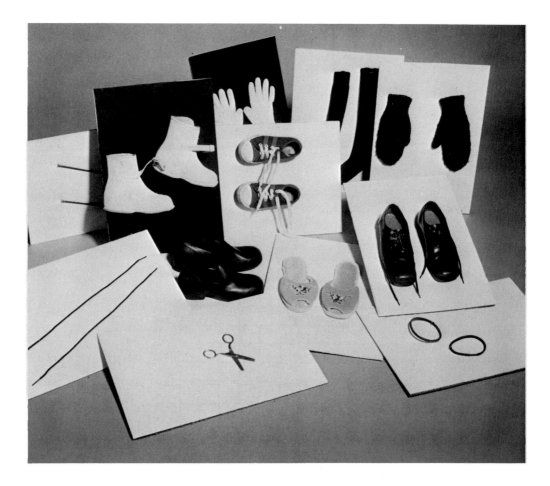

Applications

The handsome quality of this book makes it very appealing to the young child.
The familiarity of the materials here make it very appropriate for retarded children.

Variations and Related Ideas

The concept of pairs and of materials that go together can be applied to many objects in the child's classroom and home environment. The notion of left and right should also be discussed at length for the clothing items used here. Vocabulary and self-care ideas can be extended as well from the materials as the children and adults are involved with the items they encounter.

Comments

Be sure children discuss pairs when they are getting dressed and undressed at school!

68 GRADUATED LENGTHS

AREA

Intellectual: Concepts

PURPOSE

To perceive size-length differences and arrange materials using this category.

Place in Development

		Exploration	Practice	Mastery	Variations	Challenges	
							DIFFICULTY LEVELS
PHYSICAL	Fine Motor		●				
	Gross Motor						
	Practical						
PERSONAL	Self-esteem						
	Self-care						
	Creativity/ Imagination						
INTELLECTUAL	Senses/ Perception		●				
	Concepts/ Vocabulary		★				
	School Skills		●				

Other Areas: Sensory Discrimination; Physical

Specific Value

For children to comprehend fully the use of size and/or length to classify objects, they must practice often with real materials. This activity builds the child's skill in perceiving and categorizing along these dimensions. The judgments he or she makes represent an important intellectual process. The sensorimotor task stimulates and reinforces these abilities because the child sees, feels, and arranges the materials in an active, thoughtful way. Errors can be noticed by careful examination. Physical skills required in standing up the pieces are akin to those needed for any construction activity.

Child's Readiness

The large number of pieces in this activity and the perceptual and motor requirements make it a task of moderate challenge. Children who seem delighted by it are the best candidates for the learning involved.

Applications

Preschool children appreciate the challenge and satisfaction of using these sturdy materials.

Blind children can profit a great deal from the active, tactile component of this sorting task.

Variations and Related Ideas

A good deal of discussion can accompany this essentially solitary activity to extend the child's learning. The materials can also be removed from the board, traced, or used with blocks, vehicles, sand, or Play-Doh—each time reinforcing the concepts of graduations between lengths, from the shortest to the longest. Games based on the theme of changing the relative length can also be encouraged, i.e., if you move around a middle-sized piece, it becomes longer or shorter than another. All of these activities encourage cognitive processes and help the child think about mathematics and other logical operations. Similar materials are commercially available as Montessori learning activities.

Comments

Adults can spot-check on children's uses of the materials to ensure that they remain focused on size-length relations.

69 BOTTLE TOPS

AREA

Intellectual: Concepts

PURPOSE

To study and master corresponding sizes.

Place in Development

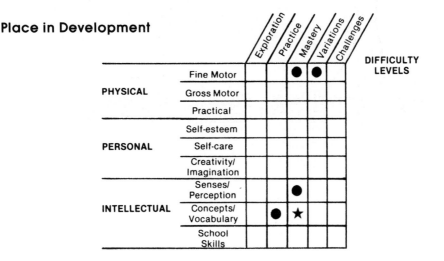

		Exploration	Practice	Mastery	Variations	Challenges
PHYSICAL	Fine Motor			●	●	
	Gross Motor					
	Practical					
PERSONAL	Self-esteem					
	Self-care					
	Creativity/ Imagination					
INTELLECTUAL	Senses/ Perception			●		
	Concepts/ Vocabulary	●	★			
	School Skills					

DIFFICULTY LEVELS

Other Areas: Fine Motor; Sensory Discrimination

Specific Value

Containers and toys tend to draw children as though they generated magnetic forces. The automatic response here is to take off and put on the lids repeatedly. In this activity the child is challenged to find the right size cap for the corresponding bottle. Motor skills are developed by the requirement that each top be turned until snug. Sensory discriminations are used in making selections among the array of objects. Mistakes are immediately corrected. The mind is active in making shifts in judgments during the entire task. The bottles are affixed to a sturdy board so that even poorly coordinated children can get involved. It is an all-around fun learning activity that even adults have been known to undertake when the children are not around!

Child's Readiness

Bottle Tops contains a moderate degree of challenge, so that children need some physical and intellectual skills if they are to succeed.

Applications

Preschool youngsters may decide this is their favorite "work" activity. Don't be surprised if you find you need two or three boards available.

Poorly coordinated and even blind children will love this manageable challenge. Confined youngsters can use it as a lap activity.

Variations and Related Ideas

The bottles in this activity are relatively small, yet each differs in some way from another. Some might even possess snap-on lids. The variations are endless. To extend the challenge, these materials could be used by a child to test his or her skills against a previous session, by time to completion, or number completed. A separate loose bottle collection could be gathered up with parents' assistance to challenge the child by using two hands and a less consistently organized array of bottles. Look for bottles of varying textures and shapes.

Comments

Unbreakable bottles are the best. Try to prevent lost lids by having a lid box nearby.

70 NUTS AND BOLTS

AREA

Intellectual: Concepts

PURPOSE

To master size relationships.

Place in Development

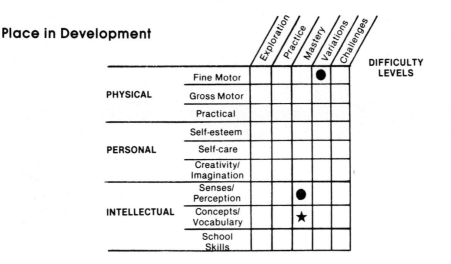

Other Areas: Fine Motor; Sensory Discrimination

Specific Value

Children are typically very interested in using adult tools and materials. It makes them feel competent and grown-up. Nuts and bolts are particularly intriguing, especially for boys who sometimes have difficulty relating to school materials that are neutral or feminine in nature. Anyone who has used nuts and bolts is aware that varying size relationships make their use somewhat of a challenge. Here, the child is required to find exactly the right nut and bolt to succeed in attaching them to the board. Physical coordination skills are also required. Once the child makes the correct discrimination, nut and bolt need to be held and turned simultaneously.

Child's Readiness

The challenge in these materials is both physical and intellectual. Children should demonstrate perceptual motor abilities such as those needed for coloring, buttoning, and using puzzles.

Applications

Older preschoolers will enjoy this real-world challenge; they can extend it to work at home.

Handicapped boys might especially enjoy this opportunity to use builder's materials.

Variations and Related Ideas

Workbench activities are very complementary to the Nuts and Bolts board. Children can use hammers, nails, saws, screwdrivers, and similar items to create designs and toys whether or not they truly resemble a real thing. This is a good opportunity as well to teach labels for the tools used by all kinds of helpers, from carpenters to bakers, firefighters, mail carriers, etc. Books can be added that describe what these persons do in their jobs. Commercial nuts and bolts, used as toys, are also available.

Comments

Large nuts and bolts are the most appropriate for children; however, a range of sizes is also important.

71 WIDE AND NARROW BOOK

AREA

Intellectual: Concepts

PURPOSE

To understand varied concepts that contribute to information and vocabulary.

Place in Development

		Exploration	Practice	Mastery	Variations	Challenges	DIFFICULTY LEVELS
PHYSICAL	Fine Motor						
	Gross Motor						
	Practical						
PERSONAL	Self-esteem						
	Self-care						
	Creativity/ Imagination						
INTELLECTUAL	Senses/ Perception						
	Concepts/ Vocabulary			★			
	School Skills			●			

Other Areas: Basic Skills

Specific Value

When children are beginning to understand how to deal with information and are collecting ideas, they need to have hands-on concrete experiences to help them take in this information fully. When ideas are presented in many different forms, the child begins to see how there is a clear relationship between them. These varied examples will help the child to understand this concept.

Child's Readiness

When the child seems to understand ideas of amount, shape, color, and size, then more abstract concepts such as wide and narrow can be discussed.

Applications

Small children will delight in the varied textures used here.
Blind children can enjoy touching and feeling these materials.

Variations and Related Ideas

You can really use your imagination to develop this box book. Any kind of real material or substance can be used. Look around; you'll find what you need in the basement, office, or a junk drawer. The children can help to select the materials, and they can then apply them to other objects all around their rooms.

Comments

Adults need to "read" this book to young children just like other books—one page at a time, with lots of discussion on each.

72 WASHER DROP AND SQUARE DROP

AREA

Intellectual: Concepts

PURPOSE

To use varied materials in sorting by size relationships.

Place in Development

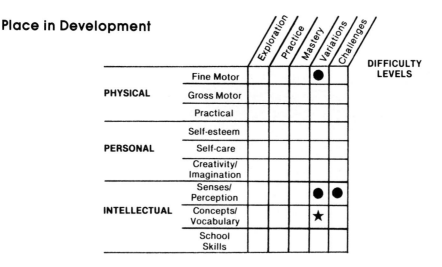

		Exploration	Practice	Mastery	Variations	Challenges	DIFFICULTY LEVELS
PHYSICAL	Fine Motor				●		
	Gross Motor						
	Practical						
PERSONAL	Self-esteem						
	Self-care						
	Creativity/ Imagination						
INTELLECTUAL	Senses/ Perception				●	●	
	Concepts/ Vocabulary				★		
	School Skills						

Other Areas: Physical; Sensory Discrimination

Specific Value

Children delight in seeing and hearing objects drop into a container. In this activity, that motivation propels them into the task of sorting squares and circles of three different sizes into a box with three different sized openings. Therefore they must see, select, and act on this perception. The task can be repeated until the child easily succeeds in sorting the shapes without errors. Most children will persist in the activity until they have achieved mastery simply because it is so satisfying.

Child's Readiness

Even children with minimal skills can achieve some success here because the materials are self-correcting; but there is a higher level of challenge in making accurate perceptions before the object reaches the appropriate one of three slots. In this sense, the Drop Boxes require moderate ability.

Applications

Little ones can try the drop boxes once they notice that different sizes are involved. Handicapped children can exercise their arms and fingers while making perceptual judgments.

Variations and Related Ideas

The materials here can be sequenced for earlier ability levels if only the smaller washers and squares are used, then each larger size added. The children will see the size distinctions when they are confronted with the tight fit of middle sized objects to the small slots. Tracing activities can be used with the circles and squares to reinforce perceptions of differences. Counting tasks and my turn-your turn games can be used as well.

Comments

Because children can sidestep the size discrimination with this activity, the adults may wish to supervise them until the notion of selected sorting and dropping is established.

73 CLOCK

AREA

Intellectual: Concepts

PURPOSE

To develop the concept of time as expressed with a clock.

Place in Development

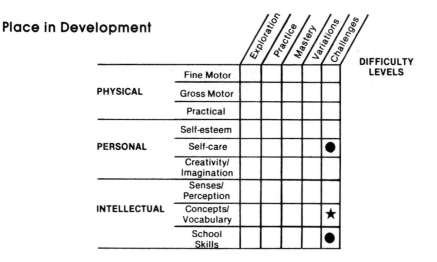

		Exploration	Practice	Mastery	Variations	Challenges	
							DIFFICULTY LEVELS
PHYSICAL	Fine Motor						
	Gross Motor						
	Practical						
PERSONAL	Self-esteem						
	Self-care					●	
	Creativity/ Imagination						
INTELLECTUAL	Senses/ Perception						
	Concepts/ Vocabulary					★	
	School Skills					●	

Other Areas: Basic Skills; Self-care

Specific Value

From early in the preschool years children deal with some concepts of time sequences, especially as they relate to daily care routines and family or school activities. The transition to using clocks, a rather abstract representation of time, is slow and difficult. The Clock, large and mounted so that it can be manipulated, enables children to examine closely how the clock moves with the passing of time. Children also need to recognize the numerals and the sets of 5 minutes between them. Here they can actually count these spaces because the clock is big enough.

Child's Readiness

This activity, while somewhat exploratory in nature, does require sufficient intellectual understandings of number and time to be used for maximum learning.

Applications

Kindergartners can benefit greatly from the study of time in this activity because they can "see" time pass.

Retarded children can examine time firsthand with the Clock. Indeed, the concrete quality of this experience is very appropriate for them.

Variations and Related Ideas

Smaller, child-sized cardboard clocks can be used along with the Clock to help children match and identify time readings. Parents can get involved at home by stating bus times, dinnertimes, and bedtimes, and pointing them out on different clocks. Digital watches should be reserved for much later so that children are not confused by the discrepant time expressions between the two.

Comments

Some caution in the use of electrical wiring is needed here. Perhaps an automatic shut-off can be installed in an extension cord. Children can also discuss the precautions they need to take with wires.

74 CALENDAR

AREA

Intellectual: Concepts

PURPOSE

To develop the concepts of days, weeks, months, and years.

Place in Development

		Exploration	Practice	Mastery	Variations	Challenges	
							DIFFICULTY LEVELS
PHYSICAL	Fine Motor						
	Gross Motor						
	Practical					●	
PERSONAL	Self-esteem						
	Self-care						
	Creativity/ Imagination						
INTELLECTUAL	Senses/ Perception						
	Concepts/ Vocabulary					★	
	School Skills					●	

Other Areas: Basic Skills

Specific Value

The concept of time periods is a difficult developmental learning task for children. They need to remember, anticipate, and organize their thinking along these dimensions. Their activities at home and school are often tied to these concepts, which are broadly used across many experiences. Teachers often use classroom calendars, but seldom are the children able to handle and study them firsthand. Here, there is the opportunity to organize a sturdy calendar. It's a valuable learning and thinking activity that involves mathematical as well as time and relational concepts. The opportunity to arrange days and weeks may build these many understandings.

Child's Readiness

Children who show signs of interest in mastering the classroom calendar will be able to derive a good deal of satisfying learning with this one.

Applications

Older preschoolers can successfully use this material once they are taught about the monthly sequences.

Deaf children might particularly appreciate exploring this activity firsthand after watching teachers use it.

Variations and Related Ideas

The children who can express their understandings of the time sequences in calendars can also apply them to weather, seasons, holidays, and past and future special events. Eventually, they may want to write down group diaries about their activities along a calendar line. Pictures and natural objects can complement their study of the characteristics of particular months and seasons.

Comments

Because there is a great deal of room for error, children will need some supervision in understanding the complex relationships in this calendar.

75 WEATHER BOARD

AREA

Intellectual: Concepts

PURPOSE

To build the concept of weather and its variations.

Place in Development

		Exploration	Practice	Mastery	Variations	Challenges	DIFFICULTY LEVELS
PHYSICAL	Fine Motor						
	Gross Motor						
	Practical						
PERSONAL	Self-esteem						
	Self-care						
	Creativity/ Imagination						
INTELLECTUAL	Senses/ Perception						
	Concepts/ Vocabulary					★	
	School Skills					●	

Other Areas: Basic Skills; Language

Specific Value

Large and sturdy representations of weather factors help children to think about this ever-present, highly variable aspect of our environment. Weather is a daily topic of conversation among people and children can participate if they have some understandings and vocabulary in this area. This activity will encourage their thoughts on the matter and help them use appropriate descriptive vocabulary. It's a wonderful contribution to their dinner conversation at home.

Child's Readiness

This activity can be used at early ability levels but if the child is independently working with it then greater understanding is needed to benefit from its use.

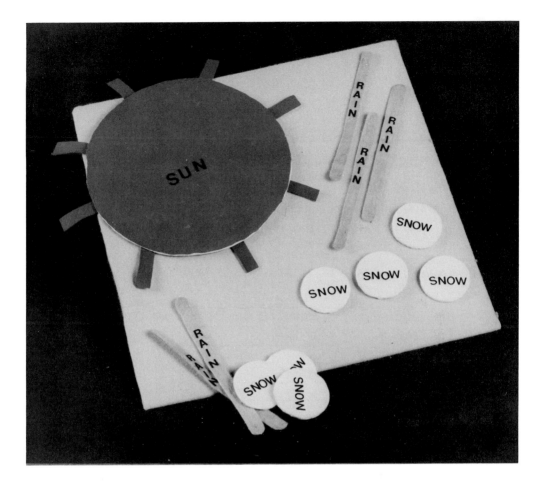

Applications

Most young children enjoy this and any other type of flannel board activity.
Any physically handicapped child can use this material easily. Language-delayed
children may particularly respond to these weather facts.

Variations and Related Ideas

Because weather is related to dressing and play activities, this activity can be
applied to the child's ongoing experiences. Records can be kept to help them understand the onset of cold or warm weather, rain or snow. Many additional resources include books, photos, and even puzzles that deal with the weather. Don't forget funny
weather-related tales from which to create illustrated stories, such as being soaked
before the bus comes or stuck in a snow mountain.

Comments

Be sure to have usable illustrations of all kinds of weather patterns.

76 AMOUNTS LOTTO

AREA

Intellectual: School Skills

PURPOSE

To explore amounts using counting and correspondence.

Place in Development

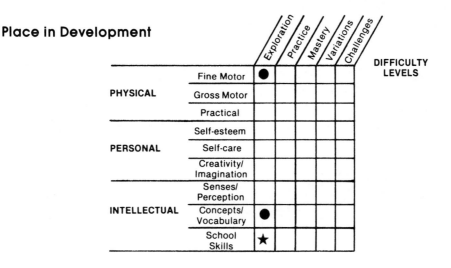

DIFFICULTY LEVELS

		Exploration	Practice	Mastery	Variations	Challenges
PHYSICAL	Fine Motor	●				
	Gross Motor					
	Practical					
PERSONAL	Self-esteem					
	Self-care					
	Creativity/ Imagination					
INTELLECTUAL	Senses/ Perception					
	Concepts/ Vocabulary	●				
	School Skills	★				

Other Areas: Concepts; Physical

Specific Value

In preparing children for premathematics and logical operations, it is important for them to learn rules of correspondence of same amounts. When they engage in counting, for example, they need to understand that one object receives one number and that counting up has to follow closely the items that are available. The Amounts Lotto develops this kind of skill and reinforces it by using eye-hand coordination to place discs in their appropriate places. It is an easily managed beginning experience in mathematics.

Child's Readiness

Children capable of matching and some simple counting will achieve a measure of success with these materials. Some physical coordination is necessary.

Applications

Preschoolers will enjoy placing these circles on the correct numbers.
Retarded children can use this activity to build counting and number skills.

Variations and Related Ideas

While one or two children can use this activity independently, they can also be encouraged by adults to express the numbers they see, first by counting and then by approximating the amounts. Once the easier and smaller numbers are mastered, children can tackle amounts up to 10. Classroom activities such as table setting, distributing papers or crayons, attendance, etc., will reinforce their understanding of amounts and correspondence.

Comments

Be sure there are the right number of loose disks so that children avoid making mistakes in using too few or too many on the board.

77 COUNTING BOOK

AREA

Intellectual: School Skills

PURPOSE

To develop and apply counting skills.

Place in Development

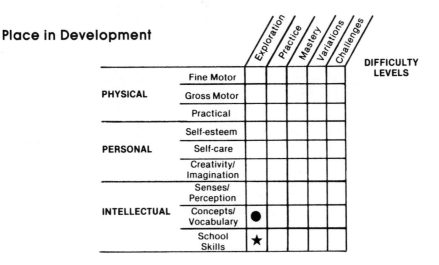

		Exploration	Practice	Mastery	Variations	Challenges	DIFFICULTY LEVELS
PHYSICAL	Fine Motor						
	Gross Motor						
	Practical						
PERSONAL	Self-esteem						
	Self-care						
	Creativity/ Imagination						
INTELLECTUAL	Senses/ Perception						
	Concepts/ Vocabulary	●					
	School Skills	★					

Other Areas: Vocabulary

Specific Value

Because learning to count is an important developmental task that requires a good deal of repetition, it helps to provide some variety for children to maintain their motivation. The Counting Book uses natural or common objects to build this skill. The items vary in size, texture, and purpose. Young children delight in being able to explore these interesting "pages" and will persist in their efforts to count using concrete items. Such exploration and practice is both enjoyable and educational.

Child's Readiness

This activity can be presented early in the child's experience if others help to maintain their focus upon carefully counting one item at a time.

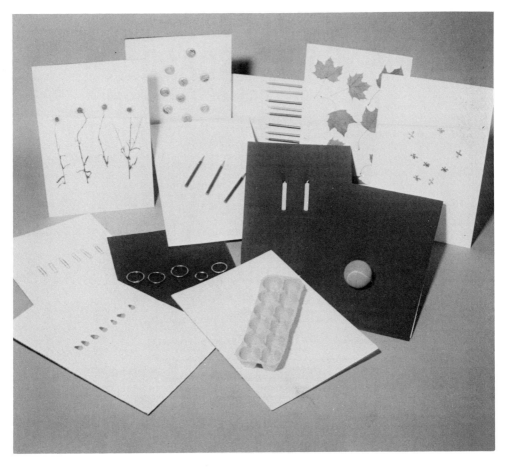

Applications

> Because it uses interesting objects, young children will be very attracted to this activity.
> Even very physically handicapped children will find these materials comfortable to use and interesting to explore.

Variations and Related Ideas

> The "pages" of the Counting Book can be arranged in a sequence or used in random fashion. Any interesting objects can be used on the pages. As children begin to understand that counting is part of the real world of things, they will almost automatically apply this to their experiences with objects at home and with other children. Counting songs and games are also very popular and a delightful way to enhance these abilities. Printed numerals can be added at a later time.

Comments

> Adults may need to make certain that missing objects do not create confusion in counting accurately.

78 SHAPES LOTTO AND SHAPES BOARD

AREA

Intellectual: School Skills

PURPOSE

To practice shape discrimination and identification.

Place in Development

		Exploration	Practice	Mastery	Variations	Challenges
PHYSICAL	Fine Motor	●				
	Gross Motor					
	Practical					
PERSONAL	Self-esteem					
	Self-care					
	Creativity/ Imagination	●				
INTELLECTUAL	Senses/ Perception	●				
	Concepts/ Vocabulary					
	School Skills	★				

DIFFICULTY LEVELS

Other Areas: Creativity; Physical; Perception

Specific Value

In their school experiences with reading and writing, children are required to make complicated discriminations between somewhat similar letters and word configurations. Practice with large shapes prior to these challenges can make later school skills a bit easier to master. In this activity children sort and match a few basic shapes (Shapes Lotto) and then a greater variety (Shapes Board). They also learn to label them repeatedly, and, in the case of the shapes and hooks, some gain practice of physical skills.

Child's Readiness

The Shapes Lotto and Shapes Board can be used early in the child's experience.

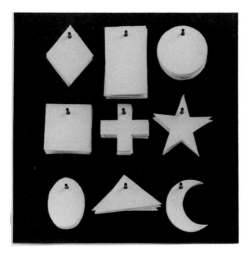

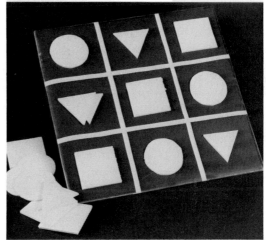

Applications

Young children will take great pride in successful sorting of these shapes.
Blind children and deaf children may enjoy the sensory and language challenges
here.

Variations and Related Ideas

Sturdy shapes are not only satisfying but they also lend themselves to use in a variety of art activities and language experiences. What's missing games or mystery bag games are very effective for reinforcing accurate perceptions and verbal descriptions of the shapes. Hidden shape activities are also quite enjoyable where additions to the line of a shape (circle into a face; square into a window) make it more difficult to perceive.

Comments

Correct labeling requires ongoing encouragement by adults as children use these materials.

79 PENNY BOARD AND PENNY BOOK

AREA

Intellectual: School Skills

PURPOSE

To practice counting skills and understand values.

Place in Development

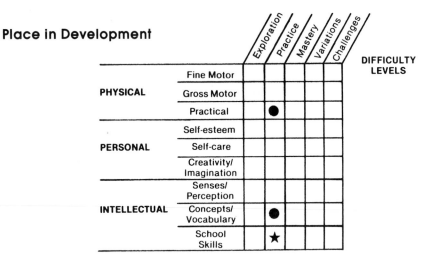

		Exploration	Practice	Mastery	Variations	Challenges	DIFFICULTY LEVELS
PHYSICAL	Fine Motor						
	Gross Motor						
	Practical	●					
PERSONAL	Self-esteem						
	Self-care						
	Creativity/ Imagination						
INTELLECTUAL	Senses/ Perception						
	Concepts/ Vocabulary	●					
	School Skills	★					

Other Areas: Concepts; Practical

Specific Value

Money concepts are exciting but difficult for children to understand. In these materials, concepts and skills are combined in the use of real money for studying amounts, numbers, and values as well as counting operations. The child can practice these abilities in a manner that is quite realistic and integrates several kinds of learning. Motivation is built-in because most children very much enjoy using real pennies.

Child's Readiness

These materials require some experience with counting and a beginning understanding concerning money values and uses. The Penny Book uses higher numbers but the Penny Board introduces numerals.

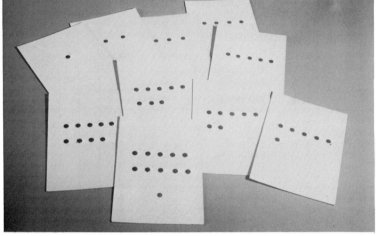

Applications

Preschoolers will enjoy the real world feeling of this activity, the grown-up sense of having real money.

Pennies may be effective in capturing the attention even of autistic or withdrawn children.

Variations and Related Ideas

While these pennies are glued on, companion cards may be used that invite the child to add the numerals or the pennies in amounts to agree. Once earlier numbers are mastered the child can continue up to 20, count by fives, or begin to consider the procedure of adding and taking away pennies to change a total. Children's penny collections at home can be used with parents to reinforce this learning.

Comments

Reminders about pennies staying out of pockets will help children resist using them for playing or keeping!

80 NUMBER WRITER

AREA

Intellectual: School Skills

PURPOSE

To practice writing numerals.

Place in Development

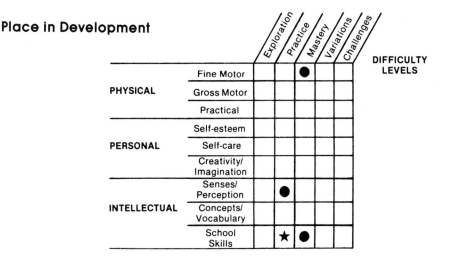

Other Areas: Physical; Self-esteem

Specific Value

Writing is a basic skill that children need to practice, yet they often make mistakes that frustrate them and others. The Number Writer is designed so that errors can be easily wiped off, yet the child is encouraged to persist in creating a legible number from a correct model. The numerals are also placed in order and a large space is allotted to each. Thus, children can feel they have room to spare while they bring their arms and fingers under greater control.

Child's Readiness

Writing readiness varies widely in children and is not always related to their ability to read them. Those who want to try writing may use this material well.

Applications

Kindergarten-age youngsters often want to rehearse these skills.
Physically handicapped children will feel greater confidence with this "mistakes OK" activity.

Variations and Related Ideas

Number writers can proceed to number 20 once children master the first numerals. Important numbers can also be used—one's age, birthdate, or the day of the month. Chalkboards are a bit more difficult but children may enjoy practicing with them. A variety of other writing media includes crayons, paint, water, or soap suds. Children may also wish to add dots to correspond with the numerals.

Comments

A soft marker or crayon makes the writing easier.

81 MAGNET BOARD

AREA

Intellectual: School Skills

PURPOSE

To study and understand science principles of magnetism and investigation.

Place in Development

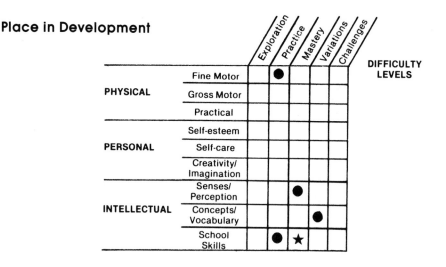

		Exploration	Practice	Mastery	Variations	Challenges
PHYSICAL	Fine Motor	●				
	Gross Motor					
	Practical					
PERSONAL	Self-esteem					
	Self-care					
	Creativity/ Imagination					
INTELLECTUAL	Senses/ Perception		●			
	Concepts/ Vocabulary			●		
	School Skills	●	★			

DIFFICULTY LEVELS

Other Areas: Concepts; Thinking

Specific Value

Children's natural curiosity forms the backdrop in science activities for their gains in understanding the world around them. Interesting objects, presented in appealing ways, stimulate the child's thinking about the why's and how's of what they see and experience in their environment. Magnetism is particularly fascinating because it appears to be magical and puzzling. Studying magnets is an excellent means of increasing knowledge at the same time that children understand the value of closely examining some feature of their surroundings in an organized way.

Child's Readiness

This material is most appropriate for children with some ability to think about abstract concepts and persist in an unstructured activity.

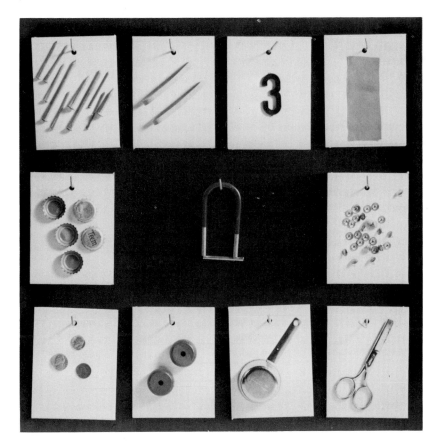

Applications

All young children enjoy the magic of magnetism; it pulls them into learning about materials and principles.

Because it is easy to use, this Magnet Board is comfortable for poorly coordinated and handicapped youngsters.

Variations and Related Ideas

Once children experiment with the variety of substances on the Magnet Board they will want to check other metal and nonmetal materials around them. Small magnets can be used in many other ways, such as fishing for paper-clipped cardboard sea creatures or using magnets under a piece of cardboard to create metal shaving designs. Many different kinds of magnets are also available in hardware stores, and children can examine varying magnets.

Comments

Be sure to explain, simply and gradually, the force that is part of how magnets work.

82 MAGNIFIER

AREA

Intellectual: School Skills

PURPOSE

To study and understand the science principle of magnification.

Place in Development

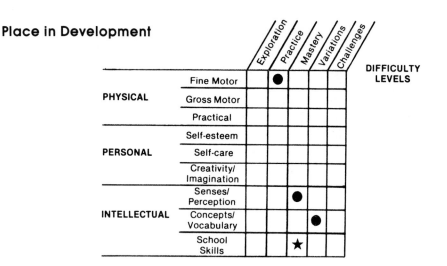

Other Areas: Sensory Perception; Vocabulary

Specific Value

In science, the process of magnification is essential to a great deal of study and investigation. Microscopes are one of science's basic tools. In this activity, children can easily work with a variety of materials under a fixed magnifying glass. They learn both about the objects themselves and what procedures to use in examining them. The reward for their careful observation is to see new and interesting features of common items. Vocabulary is also expanded through discussions and labeling about what they see.

Child's Readiness

While any child (or adult) can enjoy simply exploring the effects of magnification, more structured study and discussion creates a moderate level of challenge.

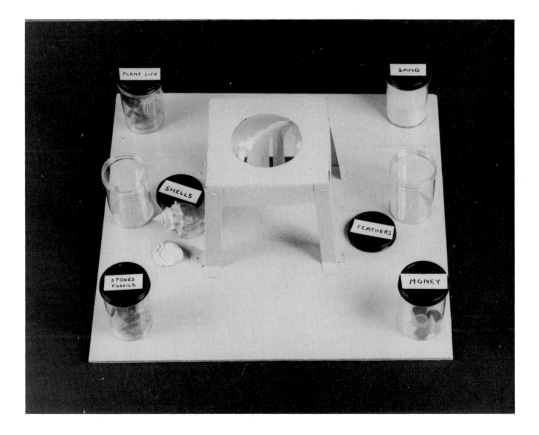

Applications

The exploration and discovery is part of the fun of this activity.

The curiosity of even the very physically handicapped youngster can be satisfied with these materials. Children with language difficulties will want to talk about what they see.

Variations and Related Ideas

The specific materials available for use with the magnifying glass can vary widely. Use your imagination! Children may wish to bring in a great many objects from home, perhaps even with a promise to report to their parents how something looked under magnification. Comparisons can be made by inspecting items that look similar yet change when seen magnified. "Fun house" mirrors might also help children to understand how images can be changed with different reflectors.

Comments

Frequent additions to the materials for use here will maintain children's motivation over a long period of time.

83 ALPHABET OBJECTS

AREA

Intellectual: School Skills

PURPOSE

To study and master some object, sound, and alphabet letter relationships.

Place in Development

		Exploration	Practice	Mastery	Variations	Challenges	DIFFICULTY LEVELS
PHYSICAL	Fine Motor						
	Gross Motor						
	Practical						
PERSONAL	Self-esteem						
	Self-care						
	Creativity/ Imagination						
INTELLECTUAL	Senses/ Perception						
	Concepts/ Vocabulary			●			
	School Skills			★	●		

Other Areas: Vocabulary; Perception

Specific Value

By far one of the most strenuous, long-term, school-related tasks of childhood is learning to read. Some of the first steps in this process are recognizing the sounds made by particular letters and identifying these with real objects and words. Because the child has regular, daily contact with the materials here it is very helpful to use them in learning. Doing so extends their understanding beyond the schoolroom. The box used to display and store the objects serves to attract the child's interest in naming the letter-words within; it also encourages independent, self-paced learning. Alphabet Objects sets can be created for many important letters.

Child's Readiness

Once children show interest in letter recognition and are able to hear initial sounds of words, they can begin studying several letters at a time using Alphabet Objects.

Applications

Older preschoolers will embrace this challenge with enthusiasm. Indeed, this is a perfectly delightful introduction to letter recognition.

A gradual, concrete introduction to reading is very appropriate here for retarded and deaf children.

Variations and Related Ideas

Popular, easy-to-hear letters are best used for Alphabet Objects. Family members can be very helpful in gathering up small items for use in the classroom and their involvement promotes a good deal of home learning as well. Once children have developed the strategy used here, picture-letter combinations can be used extensively. Eventually, simple whole words can be used—ball, car, paper—with a variety of types of these objects displayed within the box. You can even refer to it as a word store or letter box. Guessing bags can be used as well. The more words and objects (once the idea is established) the better!

Comments

Children can help each other to pronounce the letter sounds and words clearly. It's a great peer play activity.

84 SIGNS BOOK

AREA

Intellectual: Basic Skills

PURPOSE

To deal with simple abstract reading symbols in the form of familiar signs.

Place in Development

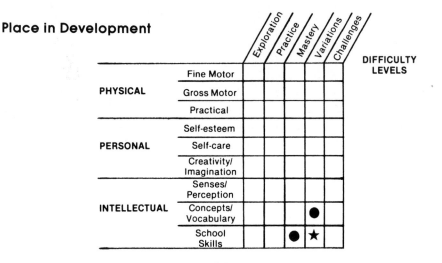

		Exploration	Practice	Mastery	Variations	Challenges	
							DIFFICULTY LEVELS
PHYSICAL	Fine Motor						
	Gross Motor						
	Practical						
PERSONAL	Self-esteem						
	Self-care						
	Creativity/ Imagination						
INTELLECTUAL	Senses/ Perception						
	Concepts/ Vocabulary			●			
	School Skills		●	★			

Other Areas: Personal: Self-esteem

Specific Value

When children are struggling with beginning mastery of some basic skills they can greatly impress themselves and others with the ability to "read" real and familiar signs. Such self-confidence may help the child to tackle additional words. These familiar word configurations also help readers to be able to decode new words. The assortment provided in this box book includes a comfortable number of words so that there is challenge—yet mastery is still within reach. These are practical words as well—useful in helping children to handle themselves in other settings. At the same time the child can easily engage grown-ups when these signs are found in public—they can talk about words and what they mean!

Child's Readiness

When the child seems to be able to differentiate one familiar word from another or remembers a word over time (including his or her own name), then this box book will be an appropriate challenge!

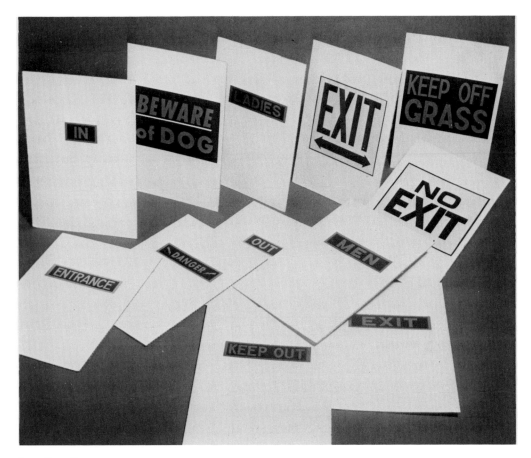

Applications

Kindergartners take a great interest in beginning reading—this sign book will be very special and inviting to use.

Retarded children need to become familiar with reading signs in public—this is a good beginning.

Language-impaired children may appreciate the opportunity to rehearse a few words repeatedly in a fun way.

Variations and Related Ideas

Once the child has comfortably mastered these words, more can be added (or problem ones removed). Try to stick to real, store-bought signs on metal or wood. Perhaps a transportation office could supply bigger street signs and a visitor to the classroom to show and tell about what signs do for us. International, nonverbal signs would be especially delightful to explore.

Comments

Adults are invited to participate. Children will appreciate your help in saying the words clearly, helping to sort mastered and challenging words, and praising the successful "reader."

85 TIMERS

Intellectual: School Skills

PURPOSE

To try different representations of time.

Place in Development

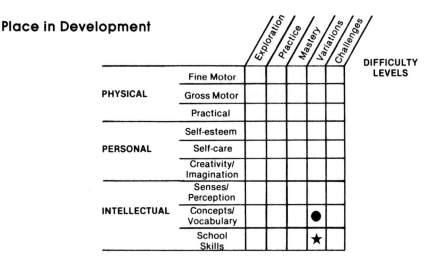

Other Areas: Concepts

Specific Value

Clocks are the most common expressions of time; but it is a challenge for children to experience other forms as well, such as the winding timer and hourglass timer presented here. The uses of time for cooking or for experiments may already be familiar to them. These extend that understanding to other kinds of activity. Timed events are part of living—from football games to long-distance telephone calls. Children gradually come to understand these notions, and using timers can help them along the way.

Child's Readiness

The activities here will require that children have some ability to deal with abstract ideas.

Applications

Just watching the timers move intrigues little ones.
The sand and clicking wheel of these timers also delight any handicapped child.

Variations and Related Ideas

Many children's games operate with timers; any puzzle or block stacking activity can be used similarly in connection with the timers. Children can eventually learn to write down how long a given activity takes with a timer. Some addition and subtraction come into play when timers are used several times or their cycles are interrupted by completion of an activity. Clocks can be used for comparisons. How about a stop-watch?

Comments

Try to incorporate some discussion about the passage of time while these timers are in operation.

86 BUCKET AND BALANCE SCALES

AREA

Intellectual: School Skills

PURPOSE

To try applying balance and weight principles to the use of measurement scales.

Place in Development

		Exploration	Practice	Mastery	Variations	Challenges
PHYSICAL	Fine Motor					
	Gross Motor					
	Practical					
PERSONAL	Self-esteem					
	Self-care					
	Creativity/ Imagination					
INTELLECTUAL	Senses/ Perception					
	Concepts/ Vocabulary				●	●
	School Skills					★

DIFFICULTY LEVELS

Other Areas: Concepts; Vocabulary

Specific Value

The notion of measurement is best expressed for children in easy-to-use scales. Because they are very action-oriented and require the child's participation, the pound scale and the balancing scale are quite effective in building understandings of weight and measurement. Children also use both visual and tactile clues to weight since they carry objects to be weighed. Their initial predictions of heaviness can be confirmed or denied with the scale; their learning then becomes useful and informative. The vocabulary of measurement, as well as that describing the objects, is also enhanced.

Child's Readiness

These materials are durable and action oriented enough to be used by very inexperienced youngsters, yet the challenge here is to "read" and possibly record the scale findings in addition.

Applications

Preschoolers like the obvious effects of heavy materials on the scales; they tip down or up rather dramatically.

Retarded children can rehearse these concepts repeatedly and in concrete ways.

Variations and Related Ideas

Depending on the classroom activities and the materials in use for other projects, children can weigh a variety of sets of objects. Grocery cans, stones, fruits or vegetables, money, wood, toys, etc., can be used—the list of items is almost infinite. The structure around these measurements can be related to other areas of the children's program to make them more meaningful. Similar activities might include lists of the actual weights or comparisons made and the names of things measured.

Comments

Continued additions of materials for the scales will maintain the children's interests over a long period of time.

87 GROCERY STORE

AREA

Intellectual: School Skills

PURPOSE

To develop the mathematical skills of numeral identification and addition in a realistic context.

Place in Development

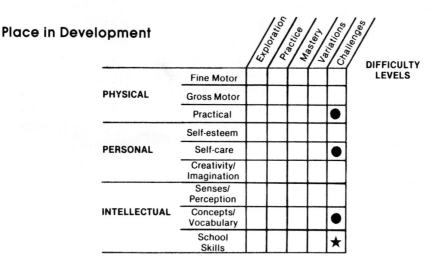

		Exploration	Practice	Mastery	Variations	Challenges	DIFFICULTY LEVELS
PHYSICAL	Fine Motor						
	Gross Motor						
	Practical					●	
PERSONAL	Self-esteem						
	Self-care					●	
	Creativity/ Imagination						
INTELLECTUAL	Senses/ Perception						
	Concepts/ Vocabulary					●	
	School Skills					★	

Other Areas: Concepts; Vocabulary

Specific Value

When children begin to study complex math operations they are dealing with rather abstract notions. To make addition more concrete, more obviously useful, the Grocery Store is an excellent learning material. Although the "prices" of the (empty or full) cans may not reflect the current rate of inflation, the numbers are nonetheless important for children who are beginning to add two or more numerals. Concepts of nutrition and some specific vocabulary can be included, as well as some early reading activities such as finding particular words on the grocery cans.

Child's Readiness

For vocabulary alone, the Grocery Store can be used early; however, for math operations, the activity is a more advanced challenge.

Applications

Kindergarten-age children delight in the social and make-believe aspects of these materials. They can learn and play store at the same time.

Physically handicapped and deaf children will appreciate the tasks here because they require few skills and are very visual.

Variations and Related Ideas

A variety of sets of materials can be used with the Grocery Store, i.e., all vegetables, all fruits, all macaroni boxes, tools, toiletries, etc. This would integrate mathematics with prereading and what might be called social studies. Children can extend the activity to pretend play using grocery bags, a cash register, and whole shelves full of empty containers contributed by mothers and fathers. A daily grocery list would require some reading as well. Small groups of children could work together, cooperating and communicating with each other.

Comments

This is a delightful curriculum boost for the latter part of the school year when children and teachers need something extra special to do!

88 BANK BOX

AREA

Intellectual: School Skills

PURPOSE

To understand and apply money concepts and addition skills.

Place in Development

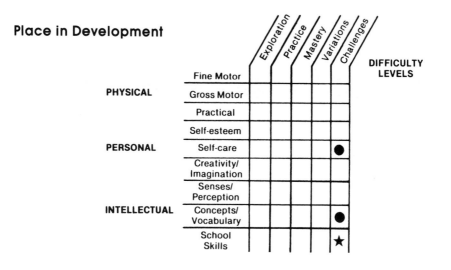

		Exploration	Practice	Mastery	Variations	Challenges	DIFFICULTY LEVELS
	Fine Motor						
PHYSICAL	Gross Motor						
	Practical						
	Self-esteem						
PERSONAL	Self-care					●	
	Creativity/ Imagination						
	Senses/ Perception						
INTELLECTUAL	Concepts/ Vocabulary					●	
	School Skills					★	

Other Areas: Concepts; Self-care

Specific Value

Children's natural fascination with money often propels them into counting and adding the bits of change they may have; but their understanding of the transformations of pennies, nickels, and dimes into one another takes a great deal of experience with real coins. It is an important developmental and learning task that the Bank Box helps to teach. Children can match the amounts on the cans to loose change available to them. The adults can check their accuracy and ask them to describe what amounts are equal to one another. In this way, they learn to master the concepts involved.

Child's Readiness

This is a rather advanced activity requiring some ability and understanding of number concepts.

Applications

Kindergarten children will relate well to this challenging task.
Retarded children can learn important practical skills with these materials.

Variations and Related Ideas

The Bank Box can be used in children's play with cash registers and paper money games. The specific amounts used can be varied to reflect whatever costs the children encounter in the real world—milk money, bus fare, a candy bar, etc. In this way they can slowly build up their understanding of how to make the amounts they need to buy things independently. The notion of banking can also be dealt with because children are often confused by how banks and merchants take money in return for an item or a figure in a passbook!

Comments

The use of real money in this activity is important, but once children can regard play money or chips as equal, they can substitute these.

SUGGESTIONS FOR CONSTRUCTION

I. PHYSICAL AREA

1 / Hanging Bracelets

Put L-shaped hooks into sturdy building blocks. Hang curtain rings or colored bracelets.

2 / Silverware Hooking

(Display Board): Screw a 12″ × 20″ board to a 6″ × 20″ base. Attach 5 L-shaped hooks. Tape plastic rings around top of knives, large and small spoons, and large and small forks.

3 / Washers for Show

Put building blocks upright and suspend assorted sized washers from L-shaped hooks. Place 2 blocks on top of each other. Suspend rubber canning rings from L-shaped hooks.

4 / Pegs in a Row

Bore 10 holes half way through a 2″ × 4″ × 20″ board for inserting dowels (1″ × 3″).

5 / Chip Drop

Attach a 2″ piece of plywood to the bottom of the open side of a 6″ × 12″ hollow block (with one side removed). Cut out slit from top of block for inserting disks.

6 / Sticks and Squares

Cut two 20″ pieces of a 2″ × 4″ board. Drill two holes in each to hold dowels (12″ long). Drill holes in squares and rectangles for placing dowels. Paint blocks and dowels matching colors.

7 / Threads and Hooks

Attach 16 L-shaped hooks to square block. Mount assorted colored spools of thread.

8 / Spoons and Brushes

Using a 6″ × 12″ hollow block, drill appropriate size holes for brushes (or spoons).

9 / Pencils in Places

Drill appropriate size holes for pencils, scissors, etc., in a 6″ × 12″ hollow block.

10 / Clothespin Stand

Attach a 4″ × 20″ base to a 10″ × 20″ piece of ¹/₈″ plywood. Apply clothespins.

11 / Dozens of Tops

Screw bottom of 12 35-mm film containers (with tops painted a different color) onto a square building block.

12 / Key Hangings

(Display Board): Screw a 12″ × 20″ board to 6″ × 20″ base. Attach several L-shaped hooks on which to mount keys.

13 / Wheel Box

Paint a wooden beverage box (one that has no sections). Mount small wheels (with cotter pins on both sides as guides) on wooden dowel. Mount on box.

14 / Bucket Ball

Materials: large plastic bucket and soft balls (basketball size) for throwing.

15 / Chime and Bell Boxes

Chime Box: Paint wooden beverage box (one that has no sections). Suspend 10 bamboo chimes by string to top of box using eyehooks. Bell Box: Paint wooden beverage box (one that has no sections). Suspend 6 large cowbells from eyehook by wire in one box and 6 small bells in another box.

16 / Baskets and Cans

Materials: peck fruit basket, supply of cans.

17 / Dropping Box

Attach a 2″ piece of plywood to the bottom of the open side of a 6″ × 12″ hollow block (with one side removed). Drill appropriate size hole for inserting bottle caps, walnuts, and chestnuts.

18 / Display Trays: Silverware, Buttons, and Pennies

Materials: 4 trays (wood or cardboard); supply of silverware, colored buttons, and pennies.

19 / Sort and Hang: Mittens, Socks, and Cloths

(Display Board): Screw a 12″ × 20″ board to a 6″ × 20″ base. Attach assorted colored mittens (socks and washcloths) to nails by plastic rings or drape hooks.

20 / Door Opener

Cut a 10″ × 12″ opening out of a 20″ × 20″ board. Attach door with hinges to board. Mount door-opening assembly to door.

21 / Door Bell

Mount doorbell and button to the front of a 20″ × 20″ board. Mount doorbell button and doorbell to front of a 20″ × 20″ board. Mount bell transformer to back of board. Wire for current.

22 / Light Switches

Toggle Switch: Mount a toggle switch and lamp base to a 20″ × 20″ board. Complete appropriate wiring on back of board. Pull Switch: Mount a pull switch socket to a 20″ × 20″ board. Complete appropriate wiring on back of board.

23 / Shoe Shop

Paint a wooden beverage box (one that comes in 4 sections). Apply label: "Children's Shoe Shop." Supply with small shoes to fit in sections.

24 / Table Setting

Divide a 20″ × 20″ board in half by using tape or felt. Glue a "perfect" complete set of tableware on half of the board. Have another complete set available to use for other half. Materials suggested: napkin, plate, knife, spoon, fork.

25 / Door and Key Latches

Cut a 10″ × 12″ opening in a 20″ × 20″ board to provide door. Mount door to a 20″ × 20″ board with hinges. Mount chain lock on opposite side.

26 / Telephone Dial

Mount telephone dial in center of a 20″ × 20″ board. Mount a 4″ × 10″ name card above dial. Mount a 4″ × 12″ card beneath dial for telephone number.

27 / Bike Lock

Mount bicycle chain lock on a 20″ × 20″ board with large screw eyes. Add card with lock combination.

II. PERSONAL AREA

28 / Me in the Mirror

Glue common hand mirror and magnifying mirror onto a 20″ × 20″ board.

29 / Right Hand-Left Hand

Cut outlines of right and left hands from plywood. Screw onto a 10″ long piece of 2″ × 4″ board. Nail onto a 20″ × 20″ board.

30 / Body Board

Screw a 5″ piece of 1″ diameter dowel from the back of the mannequin to a 20″ × 20″ board.

31 / My Health Book

Cut out 10 "pages" (12″ × 18″) of corrugated cardboard. Cover with construction paper. Glue, staple, or attach item with string or thread. Suggested items: toothbrush, tooth paste, soap, washcloth, handkerchief, mirror, hairbrush, toilet tissue, comb.

32 / Lining Up My Name

(Display Board): Screw a 12″ × 20″ piece of a ¾″ board to a 6″ × 20″ base. Screw 3½″ × 6½″ pieces of tagboard, one piece for each letter. Punch holes to insert on hook.

33 / Writing My Name

Cover a 20″ × 20″ board with clear plastic sheet. Insert child's name under plastic. Attach washcloth and plastic crayon.

34 / Writing My Phone Number

Draw lines on 20″ × 20″ white board. Cover with clear plastic. Attach "eraser" (washcloth) and plastic crayon.

35 / Zippers to Zip

Sew zippers (each with different pulls) onto 20″ × 20″ cloth. Attach to board.

36 / Fur and Buckles

Fold a 20″ × 16″ piece of fake fur so it opens in the front. Sew 4 sets of large buckles on front edges. Sew outer edge of fur onto a 20″ × 20″ cloth. Attach to board.

37 / Cup Hanging

(Display Board): Screw a 12″ × 20″ board (½″ thick) onto a 6″ × 20″ base. Screw 4 L-shaped hooks onto board.

38 / Belts and Buckles

Staple two belts (with large buckles and large holes) onto a 20″ × 20″ board. Attach bottom of buckled shoes to board.

39 / Bunches of Buttons

Sew assorted buttons onto a 20″ × 20″ cloth. Attach to board. Sew buttonholes into pieces of cloth with contrasting color.

40 / Close It Up: Grippers and Hooks

Fold and hem pieces of a 15″ × 12″ cloth so that edges meet in front. Hammer two different kinds of gripper snaps onto two pieces, and sew hooks and eyes onto three pieces. Sew outer edges of sets onto a 20″ × 20″ cloth.

41 / Lacing Vest

Cut two firm pieces of cloth (6″ × 16″ each). Using an eyelet punch, punch matching holes on each piece. Separating pieces about ¾″ from each other, sew outer piece (vertical sides only) onto a 20″ × 20″ cloth. This will make a flap for ease in lacing.

42 / Shoe Tying

Color half of white shoelace red with magic marker or dye. Fasten bottom of shoes to board.

43 / Felt Drawing

Cut assorted colors of felt into large shapes (circles, squares, etc.) "Draw" by placing pieces onto a large (20″ × 20″) piece of white felt.

44 / Nail Drawing

Using whatever pattern you wish, place nails (with large round heads) onto a ¾″ × 20″ × 20″ board. Make designs with colored string, yarn, or rope.

45 / Threading Around

Cut 12 1½″ diameter dowels in 6″ lengths. Drill a ¾″ diameter hole near top of each dowel and a ½″ diameter hole near the bottom of the dowel. Screw dowels in a circle onto a 20″ × 20″ board. Make needles by attaching one lace to a small dowel and the other lace onto slightly larger dowel.

46 / Wire Weaving

Cut out a 15″ × 15″ square from a 20″ × 20″ board. Staple hardware cloth behind "window." Drill holes onto small, round dowels to use as needles for yarn.

47 / Hole Drawing

Drill evenly spaced ½″ holes onto a 20″ × 20″ board (¾″ thick). Tie on yarn, string, or rope for "drawing" designs.

III. INTELLECTUAL AREA

48 / Fabric and Construction Circles

Cut out 9 circles (6″ diameter) of various materials and fabrics. Glue onto a 20″ × 20″ board. Suggested items: corrugated cardboard, formica, sponge, leather, cork, rubber, metal, wood, glass.

49 / Hubcap Sounds and Washboard Rhythms

Screw hubcap and washboard each onto 20″ × 20″ boards. Attach wooden spoon, thimbles.

50 / Double Chimes

Glue a 18″ square of felt onto 20″ × 20″ board. Install two sets of wood curtain rods over felt. Drill holes through rods and chimes of graduated lengths, connecting both by cord. Attach mallet and metal spoon.

51 / Light and Dark Book

Cut out 8 "pages" (12″ × 18″) of corrugated cardboard. Cover half of the board with a light shade of color (paper or fabric) and the other half with a dark shade of the same color. Suggested colors: red, yellow, orange, blue, green, brown, purple, black.

52 / Wallpaper Sorter

(Display Board): Screw a 12″ × 20″ board onto 6″ × 20″ base. Screw three L-shaped hooks for attaching matching patterns. Cut out 6 each of 3 identical patterns (4½″ × 10″) from a wallpaper book.

53 / Touch Me Board

Collect objects which are the same material, but different in "feel," e.g., rough and smooth stones, rough and smooth shells, etc. Glue rough and smooth objects side by side onto a 20″ × 20″ board. Suggested items: stones, gourds, wood, plants (teasel, grass), shells.

54 / Bells and Whistles/Kitchen Sounds

Screw or chain sound-makers onto 20″ × 20″ board. Bells and Whistles: (suggested items) bicycle bell, whistle, teacher's desk bell, wrist jingle bells, handbell. Kitchen Sounds: (suggested items) egg beater, flour sifter, potato grater, measuring spoons, teaspoon.

55 / Smell Jars

Drill holes of proper size to insert labeled plastic containers onto shelf. Using triangular support, attach shelves to a 20″ × 20″ board. Suggested items: mustard, coffee, tea, perfume, moth balls, Vicks.

56 / Taste Jars

Bore holes of proper size to insert plastic labeled containers onto shelf. Nail onto a 20″ × 20″ board. Suggested items: sugar, pepper, cinnamon, licorice, salt, hard candy (orange, cherry, mint, chocolate, lemon).

57 / Mystery Bags

Sew 6 small bags from denim. Glue or sew question mark on front of bag. Sew hem for drawstring. Fill bags with assorted objects and suspend from cuphooks. Suggested items: ping-pong balls, pennies, marbles, wood, sponge, nails.

58 / Book of Surfaces

Cut out 10 "pages" (12″ × 18″) of corrugated board. Cover with construction paper, if desired. Glue 6″ × 8″ surfaces (styrofoam, wood, etc.) onto "pages." For a glass effect, cut out a window from corrugated cardboard and tape plastic along edges. Suggested items: newspaper, corrugated cardboard, cork, rubber, glass, metal (stainless steel), wood, styrofoam, composition board, aluminum foil.

59 / Shaker Shop

Paint a wooden beverage box (one that comes in 4 sections). Place materials for shaking into plastic jars. Cover jars and set into box. Suggested items: water, beans, nails, pennies, walnuts, bottle caps, rice.

60 / Color Lotto and Color Sort

Color Lotto: Draw lines with permanent magic marker on a white-covered 20″ × 20″ board. Cut out 16 construction paper circles, 4 each of the same color. For firmness, mount circles on plastic or tagboard. Color Sort: (Display Board): Screw a 12″ × 20″ board to a 6″ × 20″ base. Cut out 36 "letters" (6 each of different colors from tagboard).

61 / Big and Small Book

Cut out 10 "pages" (12″ × 18″) of corrugated cardboard. Cover with construction paper. Glue, staple, or attach items with string or thread. Use examples of large and small. Suggested items: balloons, bottles, suckers, wood blocks, candles, peppermint sticks, safety pins, buttons, pipes.

62 / Rings n' Things

Attach 6 pegboard hooks to 20″ × 20″ pegboard. Provide supply of circular assorted items (3 to 4 each) with hole in center for placing onto hooks.

63 / Little-Lot Book

Cut out 10 "pages" (12″ × 18″) of corrugated cardboard. Cover with construction paper. Glue, staple, or attach items with string or thread. Suggested items: buttons, pine cones, gum, clothes pins, marbles, playing cards, chestnuts, peach stones, acorns, candy.

64 / Button Shop

Paint a wooden beverage box (one that comes in 4 sections). Apply label: "Button Shop." Glue colored buttons on matching painted cans.

65 / Round Book

Cut out 10 "pages" (12"×18") of corrugated cardboard. Cover with construction paper. Glue, staple or attach items with string or thread. Suggested items: record, cake tin, beret, bracelet, embroidery hoops, pot cover, buttons.

66 / Basic Shapes Board

(Display Board): Screw a 12"×20" board to a 6"×20" base. Cut 25 rectangles (3½"×6½") of tagboard. Paste 5 different black shapes on rectangles for sorting. Suggested items: squares, rectangles, circles, triangles, diamonds.

67 / Pairs Book

Cut out 10 "pages" (12"×18") of corrugated cardboard. Cover with construction paper. Glue, staple, or attach items with string or thread. Suggested items: sneakers, shoes, mittens, socks, gloves, rubber boots, books, shoe laces, scissors, stocking garters, knitting needles, house slippers.

68 / Graduated Lengths

Attach a 20"×20" board to an 8"×20" base. Screw on 4"×20" top shelf. Bore 9 round (1½") holes in one 4"×20" piece of wood, and cut 9 square holes (1¼") in another. Nail first board to top shelf and second board to base.

69 / Bottle Tops

Screw assorted sized plastic containers with tops onto 20"×20" board.

70 / Nuts and Bolts

Attach a 4"×10" board to a 4"×20" board at one end. Drill holes for inserting assorted sized nuts and bolts (5 of which go through the double thickness and 5 going through single thickness).

71 / Wide and Narrow Book

Cut out 10 "pages" (12"×18") of corrugated cardboard. Cover with construction paper. Glue, staple, or attach items with string or thread. Suggested items: wide and narrow belts, ties, rulers, chains, rugging pieces, paint brushes, ribbon, masking tape, rope, lines.

72 / Washer Drop and Squares Drop

Attach a 2" piece of plywood to the bottom of the open end of a 6"×12" hollow box (with one side removed). Washer Drop: Cut 3 slots on top side for assorted 3 sizes of washers. Squares Drop: Cut 2 slots on top for inserting large and small tiles.

73 / Clock

Screw clock onto a 20″ × 20″ board. Drill a hole through the board for electric cord.

74 / Calendar

Cut 31 pieces of plywood (2½″ square). Drill a hole in each to hang from nail on a 20″ × 20″ board. Glue a ¾″ strip to a 20″ × 20″ board for days of week. Make supply of seasons, months, and years. Drill each with two holes to hang from nails.

75 / Weather Board

Cover 20″ × 20″ board with light blue felt. Cut supply of weather shapes from felt, and label and mount on felt as desired. Suggested items: sun, clouds, rain, snow.

76 / Amounts Lotto

Paint or cover a 20″ × 20″ board with black construction paper. Make lines with white masking tape. Make supply of white disks.

77 / Counting Book

Cut out 12 "pages" (12″ × 18″) of corrugated cardboard. Cover with construction paper. Glue, staple, or attach items with string or thread. Suggested items: 1 ball, 2 candles, 3 pencils, 4 flowers, 5 notebook rings, 6 paper clips, 7 pieces of candy corn, 8 jacks, 9 bottle tops, 10 colored pencils, 11 leaves, 12 (egg carton).

78 / Shapes Lotto and Shapes Board

Shapes Lotto: Paint or cover 20″ × 20″ board with black construction paper. Make lines with white tape. Cut out 18 white squares, circles, and triangles from white tagboard or plastic. Shapes Board: Attach 9 large dowels to a 20″ × 20″ board. Cut out shapes (3 each) from plywood or tagboard. Suggested shapes: squares, triangles, rectangles, cross, oval, crescent, star, circle, diamond.

79 / Penny Board and Penny Book

Penny Board: (Display Board): Screw a 12″ × 20″ board to a 6″ × 20″ base. Attach 5 L-shaped hooks. Cut out 15 rectangles (3½″ × 6½″) from tagboard. Glue 1 to 5 pennies on each rectangle (each appropriately numbered). Punch holes for inserting on L-shaped hooks. Penny Book: Cut out 10 "pages" (12″ × 18″) of corrugated cardboard. Cover with white construction paper. Glue 1 to 10 pennies on each page.

80 / Number Writer

Attach 20″ × 20″ white linoleum to board. Make lines with black tape. Put sample numbers on top row of board. Attach "eraser" (washcloth) and plastic pencil.

81 / Magnet Board

Apply L-shaped hooks to a black 20″ × 20″ board. Cut out 10 rectangles (4″ × 5″) and punch holes. Use glue to attach suggested items: nails, bottle caps, coins, wooden bead, stainless steel cup, scissors, thumb tacks, fabric, plastic-coated number "3," needles.

82 / Magnifier

Mount large magnifier on 20″ × 20″ board at proper height to view various objects. Glue plastic jars with examples to be observed. Suggested items: plant life, sandpaper, coins, fossils, feathers, shells, stones.

83 / Alphabet Objects

Paint a wooden beverage box (one that comes in 4 sections). Apply label: "B." Suggested items: bell, balloon, ball, brush, belt, book, bracelet.

84 / Signs Book

Cut out 10 "pages" (12″ × 18″) of corrugated cardboard. Cover with white construction paper. Glue on commercial signs. Suggested signs: In, Beware of Dog, Ladies, Men, Exit, Keep Off Grass, Entrance, Danger, Out, No Exit, Keep Out.

85 / Timers

Screw Presto timer and egg timer onto a 20″ × 20″ board.

86 / Bucket and Balance Scales

Bucket Scale: Attach a 20″ × 20″ board to a 10″ × 20″ base. Screw a 2″ × 4″ board onto top of board. Suspend scale (up to 25 pounds) from cup hook. Balance Scale: Screw a 4″ × 20″ shelf onto a 20″ × 20″ board to support plastic containers. Attach 1″ square × 4″ piece of wood under center of shelf for balance scale. Suggested items: nails, corn, sawdust, ping-pong balls, rice.

87 / Grocery Store

Paint a wooden beverage box (one that comes in 4 sections). Apply label: "City Supermarket." Put prices on canned goods.

88 / Bank Box

Paint a wooden beverage box (one that comes in 3 sections). Apply label: "U.S. Savings Bank." Glue 1 penny, 5 pennies, and 1 nickel; 10 pennies and 2 nickels; and 1 dime onto white cans.